J

GW00360746

The Dog in the Family

THE DOG IN THE FAMILY

by Stanley Dangerfield

with contributions by Dr. A. D. Walker
and S. F. J. Hodgman, M.R.C.V.S.

POPULAR DOGS · LONDON

Popular Dogs Publishing Co. Ltd
3 Fitzroy Square, London W1

An imprint of the Hutchinson Group

London Melbourne Sydney Auckland
Wellington Johannesburg Cape Town
and agencies throughout the world

First published 1973
© Spillers Foods Ltd

Set in Monotype Ehrhardt
Printed in Great Britain by
Ebenezer Baylis & Son Ltd,
The Trinity Press, Worcester, and London

Produced by Hutchinson Benham Limited

ISBN 0 09 118080 5

Contents

List of Illustrations

Photo credits: The Central Press Photos Ltd., 3a; The Guide Dogs for the Blind Association, 2a; London Express News and Feature Services, 4a; By kind permission of the Metropolitan Police, 2b; Derek Roe, 1; Spillers Ltd., IVb, 9. All other photographs by Sally Anne Thompson.

Drawings by Shireen Faircloth

1 | The Dog in the Family

If you don't like dogs the time to stop reading this book is now. If you carry on one or two awful things can happen. First you might become bored, even offended, because this is written by one who unashamedly does like dogs. Moreover he not only likes them, but admires and respects them.

The other thing that can happen is that you might become converted to dog ownership and I would certainly not want that to happen in this way. It is no part of my ambition to 'sell' the idea of dog ownership to those not already converted. And the best salesman I know is the dog in general and a puppy in particular. From which it follows that I believe that unless the soulful eyes, the merry wagging tail and the mixture of high spirits and quiet devotion found in almost every dog are sufficient to persuade you to keep one of these animals, then you will be better off without. Moreover, and I shall make this point many times during the course of this book, the dog would be better off without you.

While nobody knows the exact number of dogs there are in Great Britain, the figure is usually assessed at something approaching five millions. Inevitably, there is some sort of guess-work involved in this because we do not have to declare dogs on our census forms. We must therefore work from the only known figures which are the licences issued. These are in the region of three millions. Added to this there are all of the puppies under six months of age which are not required to be licensed and additionally all of the farm dogs, guard dogs, guide dogs, police dogs, etc. which are also excused licensing. Over and above this there must be a large army of dogs whose owners have conveniently forgotten to take out a licence! Whatever the precise figure is, however, it is remarkably high and is commonly, although erroneously believed to be the highest number of dogs per head of population of any country in the world. Oddly enough statistics suggest that this record is in fact held by the Americans.

That aside, the number of dogs owned is sufficiently high to hammer home the oft-made point that the dog is nearer to the heart of man than all other animals. A similar claim can be made by horse lovers but it bears little investigation merely because although a horse may have a place in our hearts, very rarely does it have a place in our home. Conversely the overwhelming majority of dogs in Britain are in every sense home dogs – that is family dogs and perhaps even more precisely dogs who are members of the family.

The reason for this is not hard to see. Dogs are the most interesting of all the animals for the good and simple reason that they are the only ones we can hope to understand. We have lived with them for so long that we can read their every mood at a glance. Admittedly, except for a few experts, this ability to read them is usually restricted to the owner of the dog and in that case it is very simple. We can tell by the expression of their ears, their eyes and their tails just when they propose to be naughty, nice or dumbly unco-operative. We can tell when they are pleased and even more easily when they are angry. They tell us almost as if they used words when they are hungry or when they need water, when they are tired or when they are frightened. While they are incapable of true deceit, they do occasionally attempt to pull our legs a little. For example by limping long after the passing pain of a minor injury has been forgotten.

The dog then is unique. And that because it is the only animal we not only welcome to our hearth and home determined to cherish and protect for the remainder of his days, but one of which we ask nothing in return except that it should be a companion.

But although we ask nothing, in fact we receive numerous benefits. First of all we get a loyalty and devotion which it is impossible to buy. Which indeed we do not even have to earn. It is a remarkable and in many ways a sad fact that even the ill-treated and abused dog invariably loves its owner as much, perhaps even more, than one who is guarded, cossetted and cherished.

Apart from this there are practical advantages. We live in a lawless age and there is no indication that this position will improve in the immediate future. At times like this a dog is more than just a companion, he is a guard. Almost inevitably when the word 'guard' is mentioned some think of a big and savage dog that will fight with tooth and claw in defence of its owner. I think of no such animal. Indeed I will go as far as to say nothing would persuade me either to own such a dog myself or to recommend anybody else to acquire one. There are far too many hazards attached to the ownership of a savage dog. While it is perfectly simple to train any dog to be aggressive and indeed to provoke them into acts of violence, it is a very different thing to stop them once they have started. This frequently proves too difficult for the pet owner and the result is that some law-abiding citizen making a legitimate call at a house is attacked and bitten, perhaps badly. It hardly needs to be mentioned that the end of this sort of incident can result in the dog being destroyed, either by the choice of the owner or occasionally by the insistence of the courts. Even more hazardous is the fact that children, perhaps friends of the owner's youngsters, are unwittingly bitten.

In my opinion a dog's guarding role is best carried out by his mere presence. Like the atom bomb he is a deterrent. While most of us know that, for example, a pet Labrador is unlikely to bite an intruder, the intruder is by no means as certain of this. Who could blame him? What is more the unwelcome visitor's mere shiftiness, aggression, or fear, provokes some reaction in even the most mild and well mannered dog. Even if he does not rush into attack, and one would certainly hope that he would not, he becomes wary, his hackles rise; perhaps his lips curl back. And even if the change in character is not as marked as this, he will become quiet, deliberate in his movements and certainly behave in a way that few strangers would dare to ignore.

Even more important than this, there is the fact that the dog gives tongue. When a dog is in the house, and no intelligent pet owner would keep one anywhere else, he listens all the time. Anything unusual will wake him instantly. Foot-falls in the dark will tell him exactly what is going on outside. He would hear the slightest scratch at a window, the touch of a lock when it had been preceded by unfamiliar footsteps. An attempt to 'case the joint' by a would-be housebreaker would be noticed by the dog. And in all these instances the dog would do what comes naturally to him. That is bark.

Now the one thing all minor criminals are very much afraid of is a barking dog. To some extent of course, they fear that they may be bitten. But there is something far more important than this. What they really fear is detection and capture, and therefore at the first hint of noise in a house they move on to somewhere where their risks are likely to be less. While there undoubtedly have been some burglaries perpetrated on houses in which there were dogs, it is undeniable that it is much more normal for houses which have even small dogs to be left severely alone.

As an aside there was some amusing correspondence in *The Times* recently on this subject. The first writer of a letter to the editor suggested that as old people were often in need of assistance, they should be given a free telephone. A second writer suggested that they would be much better off with a dog. A third writer, while agreeing that this was a good idea from the point of view of companionship, made the point that you could not use a dog to ring up the police in the event of an unwelcome caller. And the fourth writer capped the lot by saying that he had never heard of a telephone which was sufficiently perceptive or physically capable of barking before the unwelcome visitor had the chance to commit an offence and thereby discouraging him from so doing!

But perhaps it would not be correct to over-stress the question of a dog being required for protection since not everybody is in need of it and for that matter not everyone is old! Some are both young and the parents of young families. But here again there is a benefit. There can be no doubt that it is an enormous advantage for young children to be brought up in the same house as a dog. Right from the start they learn not to be afraid of dogs, which fact alone makes them less rather than more likely to be bitten. They also learn the all important principles of service. We human beings in this comparatively affluent country take much for granted and there is always a risk of us taking, or at

least expecting, even a little more than that! But we know from experience that we must give as well as take. And what could be better than that this lesson should be instilled into children while they are in their young and formative years. With a dog around the house, they soon learn that a dog is dependent. Dependent upon humans for grooming, exercising, feeding and watering. They know that they must accept responsibility and this lesson frequently stands them in good stead in later life.

They may also learn some of the facts of life in a mild and harmless way. It must surely be better for young children to learn of the beauties and mysteries of procreation by a sight of their own pet giving birth to and rearing puppies than by acquiring dubious and doubtful information of a similar nature behind cupped hands and accompanied by a welter of smirking and giggling.

Perhaps at this point I have exceeded my brief and started to persuade the non-dog owner to change his position. However that was not my intention and I repeat that nobody should have a dog unless they feel they cannot do without one. Dog ownership is a partnership and unless there is mutual attraction, the partnership cannot be profitable.

And to end this chapter a simple ten-point charter for the would-be dog owner. All of these things will be enlarged upon during the course of the book but if at a glance through these you do not think that you are capable of following this charter, it may help your decision on whether or not you should own a dog:

1. *Talk to dogs:* Not baby talk or childish chatter, but ordinary conversation. Animals like to hear you speak to them although they will never learn to answer.

2. *Adopt a regular routine:* All pets, and particularly dogs, appreciate this. Feed and water at the same time each day. Let them anticipate their exercise periods and know when they have to get up and when to go to bed. They have a built-in clock which tells them when certain things should happen, so don't upset their simple time-table and pleasures.

3. *Give them company:* Certainly they may occasionally be left for a few hours, but equally certainly not all day and every day. If nothing else they can be given the company of their own kind.

4. *Give them playthings:* Animals, having uncomplicated minds, like toys to play with. For dogs, an indestructible ball or ring.

5. *Provide fresh air:* They cannot be really healthy or happy without it. They can go out in the sunshine as long as it is not wet and freezing. Hot, airless, stuffy rooms make them dull and lethargic.

6. *Keep them healthy:* If you suspect they are ill or in pain, call in your veterinary surgeon. A stitch in time saves nine.

7. *Learn something about them:* The more you know about animals the easier it is to look after them. Specialist books about dogs of all the many breeds are available at modest prices.

8. *Train and discipline them:* This sounds harsh, but it's the reverse. A trained animal is confident and sure of itself because it knows what is expected of it.

9. *Don't kill them with kindness:* The surest way to shorten dogs' lives is to over-feed them. Too much food, too many titbits, sticky biscuits and chocolate ruins both health and waistlines.

10. *Save them from suffering:* When the day comes that illness or accident means that they have only poor health and pain to look forward to, take the hard way out and save them further suffering. It's man's opportunity to forget his own feelings and prove his true love of animals.

2 | The Background of Dogs

It is very simple to keep a dog. Indeed it may be too simple, a fact which persuades some people to enter into it without sufficient prior thought. In many cases, those who enter a commitment as lightly as this survive the experience with no lasting ill effects. Occasionally, however, they come unstuck. There are so many ways in which this can happen that there is little point in enlarging on them now. But merely to make this point: an ageing person living in a small fourth-floor flat might buy a cuddly, young Saint Bernard puppy without facing the obvious truth that it will grow into a mature and manifestly unsuitable adult. There are countless variations on this theme.

All of these animals grow up to become 'problem dogs', a handy title which disguises the fact that it is really a simple case of a problem dog owner! Either way it's immaterial, because 'problem dogs', whether that problem be one of size, shape, coat, temperament or health, require problem solvers. And so a wealth of information is made available as to just how all these many problems can be overcome.

The result is that the impression is planted in some people's minds that keeping, rearing, feeding and educating a dog is a vastly complicated exercise necessitating intense study and frequent reference to a battery of textbooks. This is false, and I repeat that this exaggerated view should never be taken of what is essentially a question of common sense. Dog keeping is not an art form, a science nor yet a seven-day-a-week chore. It is a simple pastime which brings an enormous amount of pleasure in response to a surprisingly small amount of trouble.

Indeed I feel the only thing a potential dog owner, or indeed an existing owner, can do wrong is to forget that their dog is a dog. It is not a small human being with four legs covered by a stretched dog skin. It is a dog. Dog all the way through. It has the breeding of a dog. The background and history of one. It has a dog's thought processes and behaviour patterns. It is, and will remain, a dog.

That being so we could all profitably spend a few moments learning something about the dog as a species. While not intended to be exhaustive what follows in this chapter is at least an introduction to this remarkable animal. An introduction, which it is hoped having been read and then preferably relegated to the back of the reader's mind, may help him or her to stay on the right lines for the duration of their own particular human/dog partnership.

It is generally accepted that many millions of years ago the dog started off in this world looking something like a tadpole. Since most other mammals started off in a similar way there is no reason to believe that the dog was any exception. I do not think this of any great interest to an owner of a present day dog. Still less do I think it of interest that having skipped a few million years we should waste too much of our time deciding whether a dog is a descendant of the wolf, a jackal, a fox, a dhole, a dingo or any other one of half a dozen similar animals. The probability is that it developed side by side with all of these other animals which means that neither one is a direct ancestor or descendant of the other but that they were all

cousins which slowly developed on different lines. Much more to the point is the established fact that the dog as we know it today certainly existed many thousands of years ago although at that time he was of course a wild or at least a semi-wild animal. He was also, and this point needs to be made now although I shall return to it, a pack animal. That means that he spent all of his time within the confines of a pack and rarely showed any taste for solitude. The cat may walk alone but never, willingly, the dog. This pack existence made it possible for him to live because he was a hunter fighting for every mouthful of food that he ate to keep him alive. One doubts whether the life was particularly rewarding and certainly it could not have been easy. But to suggest from this that the dog's mentality was such that he looked around for an easier way of existing and deliberately threw in his lot with man is an over simplification.

Much more likely is the theory that this association grew slowly, gradually and perfectly naturally. That is to suggest that originally dogs hung around the dwellings of prehistoric man because they found that there was a certain amount of scavenging to do which enabled them to live off the scraps rejected by cave dwellers. They would of course still be frightened or rather wary of man but nevertheless they gave him a certain protection because dogs, being what they are, would act, if not exactly as guards, then certainly as sentinels because they would give warning of the approach of wild animals.

Another thing which would follow naturally is that they should, while keeping a wary distance, follow the man on his hunting expeditions. At the time of a kill, once again there would be pickings; some of the intestines, maybe the skin, perhaps the head, would be rejected and the dogs would stay on for a feast after man returned to his cave. The brighter dogs would probably take a step forward and help actively in the hunt, partly through excitement and perhaps because they learned that man was more adept at killing than themselves and so more likely to provide them with a regular meal. When the Stone Age man had become less nomadic, the dogs lived round the village and in time it is almost inevitable that an occasional puppy, perhaps an orphan, would be taken indoors as a child's plaything. In the course of time some must have proved that a tame dog was a far more useful hunting assistant than one which was half wild and a natural enemy. From then on the partnership would make progress, if not year by year, then certainly century by century and once again, almost inevitably, this in time would lead to a process of selective breeding. This is not to suggest that it had at that time any such high flown title. Even so, even the most primitive man must have realized that if he wanted a hunting dog, he needed one which was sleek and long legged. If he wanted a guard then size, strength and substance was important. If he wanted a dog which would go underground then once again he had to consider smaller dogs which in time would develop into the little terriers we know today. And so slowly there grew up not merely an affinity between man and dog but the desire to own dogs built to a certain size and shape and possessed of a precise and particular temperament.

Although dogs started as the companions of men almost as poor as himself, it does not appear to have been very long before he was promoted to being the friend of kings and queens! Whenever the activities of royalty have been chronicled throughout the ages, there is frequent mention made of a dog. For example, Homer describes the return of Ulysses after twenty years. He was in disguise but his old dog Argus knew him. Although too old and ill to move, the dog wagged his tail, drooped his ears and fell dead. Another tells that King Lysimachus' favourite dog was 'Hyrcanus'. When the King was killed fighting for Alexander the Great, the dog stood by the funeral pyre and as the flames reached their height 'gave one bound into their midst and perished with his master'.

King Arthur's favourite dog is mentioned by Tennyson in the *Idylls of the Kings* as follows:

> 'And while they listened for the distant hunt,
> Chiefly for the baying of Cavall,
> King Arthur's hound of deepest mouth. . . .'

Queen Elizabeth I had a toy terrier, while Mary Queen of Scots owned a little dog so faithful that it is said to have followed her to the scaffold by hiding under her skirts. King Charles II was rarely seen without his favourite toy spaniels, a breed which bears his name to this day. James II also liked this breed and even

Charles II with his spaniel

took them on naval engagements. Frederick, Prince of Wales, was given a dog by Alexander Pope with the inscription: 'I am His Highness's dog at Kew; Pray tell me sire, whose dog are you?'

Coming even more up to date, Queen Victoria had more dogs of more breeds than any other monarch before or since. Queen Alexandra also took a keen interest in dogs and showed many,

including Pekingese, Clumber Spaniels and Borzois. Edward
VII's favourite was a Wire-haired Fox Terrier who followed the
pall-bearing gun carriage at his master's funeral. On his collar
was engraved: 'I am Caesar the King's dog'.

The dogs of modern royalty are almost too well known to
need comment. There were the Labradors of King George VI,
the Dachshund of the Queen Mother, the Pugs of the late Duke
of Windsor and the Cavalier King Charles of Princess Margaret
and last, but by no means least, those Corgis who share the lives
of Her Majesty the Queen and the Duke of Edinburgh.

Considering how long dogs have been so close to men, and
important men at that, there are surprisingly few monuments to
them. Such few as there are have become well known. Memorials
are quite naturally more plentiful, but almost invariably un-
recorded since they are frequently sited in owners' gardens or
dogs' cemeteries rather than in prominent and public positions.

'Greyfriars Bobby' is perhaps the best-known dog to earn a
permanent memorial. Admittedly the range of his fame springs
more from Walt Disney's film than the little statue in Edinburgh.
But possibly the film would never have been made had the statue
not existed. 'Bobby' was a Skye Terrier and the inscription on the
monument says he 'followed the remains of his master to this
churchyard in 1858 and refused to be separated from the spot
until he died'.

Fontainebleau is a memorial to a dog called 'Bleau', who was
present when his master injured himself in what was then a forest.
The dog, it is said, realized his master's need and located and
scratched for water from an underground stream. The man later
bought the forest, erected a fountain on the spring site and called
it Fontainebleau.

In north Wales there is an inscription on a stone to a Deerhound, 'Beth Gelert', accidentally slain by his master the Welsh
Prince Llewellyn who thought the dog had killed his child whereas
in fact he had killed a wolf who was attacking the infant.

In Guzerat there is a stone tribute to 'Carlos', a Retriever who
followed his master, Sir W. Knott, all through the Afghan
campaign. 'Igloo', a little mongrel, has a monument in Pine
Ridge Cemetery, Boston. He accompanied Commander Byrd on
his expedition to the South Pole in 1928. The inscription reads:

THE BACKGROUND OF DOGS 23

'He was more than a friend'. Sir Walter Scott wrote the following words carved underneath a monument to a favourite Deerhound:

> 'Beneath the sculptured form which late you wore
> Sleep soundly "Maida", at your master's door'

'Obo', the forerunner of all American Cocker Spaniels, is remembered by a small plaque. 'Jock of the Bushveld', a Bull Terrier, has a road in the Transvaal named after him. A Foxhound buried in Euston Park, England, is remembered by:

> 'Foxes rejoice, here lies buried your foe.'

Finally, there is the monument erected by Lord Byron, in memory of 'Boatswain', a Newfoundland. The inscription is lengthy. One part reads:

> Near this spot
> Are deposited the remains of one
> Who possessed beauty without insolence
> Courage without ferocity
> And all the virtues of man without
>   his vices.

But in spite of our long association we still do not know everything about dogs. We do not, for example, know whether in addition to the five senses we possess, those of sight, taste, smell, hearing and touch, they have a mysterious extra. A sixth sense. Common sense says No. And the more one knows about animals the more readily explained is some of their puzzling behaviour.

True stories of the uncanny way in which mountain dogs move to safety just before an avalanche crashes down can be explained by their acute sense of hearing which detects the cracking and rumbling, even the small trickle of stones which must precede a major fall. Additionally, they feel the disturbances in the earth's surface through their pads.

During the war trained dogs found people buried beneath tons of fallen masonry, ignoring the dead and pointing only to the living. Uncanny until we remember that their sense of smell is many hundred times more delicate than that of a human being. We know they can detect the presence of metallic mines buried many feet below ground. We know they can tell by a sniff at our clothing just how many dogs we have been speaking to. I have

The Prior of the St. Bernard Hospice with Leon, who saved thirty-five lives

heard my dogs bark when a cat tip-toed past the door, and seen a R.A.F. dog dash straight to a man hidden in a four-acre field. But in each case I saw their nostrils tremble first, indicating that smell was the secret.

Why then complicate a simple issue. Why not admit that all their senses are more finely developed and that dogs which meet their masters at the gate do so because their hearing is so finely tuned that hundreds of yards away they can not only pick out the exhaust note of his make of car, but distinguish between that and the hundreds of similar models on the road?

There is one phenomenon which remains unexplained. That is the homing instinct. Dogs which have been taken scores, even hundreds of miles by car frequently head straight off in the direction of home, over ground they have never covered before. In these cases there is no question of memory playing a part, nor yet of help from eyes, ears, pads, tongues or noses. What is left but a sixth sense?

Having admitted that there is one big field in which we know nothing about dogs it might be considered presumptuous to write on the mind of a dog. But, oddly enough, here we are on

much surer ground because although dogs cannot speak, a lot
has been learned about their thought processes by scientific
tests and man's observation.

We know for example that they cannot recognize colours.
This was established through tests designed to measure hearing.
When a hungry dog sees food his mouth waters. Thus a dog could
be trained to salivate by sounding the same musical note as he
received his daily meal. After a week the note alone makes his
mouth water because of the association with food. This
established, his skill at distinguishing one note from another was
tested. It was found dogs could easily distinguish between two
adjoining notes and even between notes a quarter of the normal
distance apart!

Similar experiments have shown dogs are brilliant at deciding
where sounds come from. They were sat inside a circle of card-
board screens and given food when they ran to whichever made
a buzzing noise. Soon they could precisely locate sound from
thirty-two possible sources.

Attempts to make dogs salivate by displaying different colours
failed. Similarly dogs proved unable to distinguish different
colours on boxes containing their dinner. This suggested that
dogs are colour blind and probably cannot even see colours. So
if your dog is bored by your black dress or dark suit but excited
by your tweed or corduroy trousers, it is not colours which tell
him your plans. He probably knows whether he is coming with
you or not by some revealing but unsuspected mannerism.

Here's an example from my own experience. I have a first
floor office and a habit of walking round the garden in search of
inspiration. Thus I go downstairs and out of doors twenty times
a day. These expeditions are ignored, yet a longer trip to the post
office or shop produces a dog at my heels! It's not very difficult
for a dog. Mine realizes that when I am leaving the house I
always pick up the car keys; the little jingle tells my dog it's
worth coming. You probably have similar habits which make
life easier for your dogs. They are very observant but only notice
the things which affect them.

Their sense of hearing is almost beyond human understanding.
Imitate, no matter how exactly, your husband's dog-calling
whistle and your pet will totally ignore it.

Scent is equally remarkable. A dog can track a man through a field crossed by dozens – even hundreds – of other men. He can still do it a day, two days, or even four days later. He can decide from among a dozen similar articles the one you have touched. Scent explains why belligerent dogs threaten those who are afraid of them; why they run past your house-cat and chase one of a similar size, shape and colour.

All this means three things; dogs are more observant than humans, their hearing is better developed and their sense of smell near perfect.

While appreciating these differences, we overlook others. Some owners, deciding that their dog is 'almost human' are disappointed to find that he has different moral values. Take stealing: accept that a dog cannot steal – he merely takes food. We can teach him that we are displeased if he takes food, and thereafter he is ashamed if we catch him at it! But he has still not absorbed our standards of guilt. He's merely decided to abide by our ridiculous rules!

To a dog it is not disgusting to be sick indoors. There is something he does not want in his tummy so he brings it up. He has no sense of shame about it. Mud on the floor means nothing to a dog, neither does mud on your best clothes. Going off after a girl-friend brings no remorse. We must accept that dogs do not feel shame for human reasons although we can still train them to obey our rules.

Finally we should always remember that dogs have a deep-rooted pack instinct. Long before they became domesticated, they fought, lived, hunted and loved in packs. They will still do these things if given the opportunity. All packs have a leader who demands and receives blind obedience. Junior pack members accept and welcome this fact. They have the instinctive knowledge that the pack will perish unless it remains united.

The modern equivalent of the pack is your family. The pack leader who expects and receives from the dog the centuries old unhesitating obedience is you. Not very flattering perhaps. You probably assumed that the dog thought you were God. In truth, he merely thinks you are a better dog than himself!

3 | Choosing a Breed

Before you can choose a puppy you have to choose a breed. And there's a very wide choice. The Kennel Club has well over a hundred different breeds on its registers and above that there are the 'non admissibles' such as Border Collies, Heelers and Jack Russells. On top of that the biggest single 'breed' in the country: the Mongrel, or if you prefer a more polite title, although in truth it means the same thing, the Cross-bred. Every single one of these breeds is suitable for someone. But equally certainly, not every single one of them is suitable for you. You must make a choice.

By the very nature of things, that choice will almost certainly be influenced by somebody else's dog. Few decide to buy a breed merely by reading an account of it. They either see a picture, or much more probably a living dog and become attracted to it. This means that the more popular a breed is the greater its 'exposure', and from this the likelihood that it will become even more popular.

This is in many ways regrettable as it leads to a blind follow-my-leader choice, ignoring the fact that a breed which suits a pop star or politician may not suit others. Neither for that matter might the breed which every other person in your road keeps and lives with in perfect harmony.

While fashions in dogs are often believed bad and a certain forerunner of 'ruination of the breed' I feel the real risk is much greater. A glance at the top dogs over the last fifty years is revealing. From 1920 to 1925 the volatile Wire-haired Fox Terrier ruled the roost. In 1926 he was toppled by the Alsatian who was king for a mere two years until adverse publicity set him back. Then came the twenty-year reign of the Cocker Spaniel, in turn upset in 1954 by the Miniature Poodle. Ten years later he was dethroned by the Alsatian's defiance of the dictum 'Champions never come back'.

So we have the odd position that those who owned only the most fashionable breeds during this period, and doubtless many thousands did, would have owned in turn a Fox Terrier, Cocker Spaniel, Poodle and Alsatian. It would be difficult to imagine a more diverse selection. Indeed few people who could ever be really happy with any one of them could hope to be even reasonably content with any of the others. So much for a blind following of fashion.

Since some, however, want to play follow-my-leader and others are equally anxious to avoid it, I have listed below the top twenty breeds for the years 1970, 1971 and 1972 which might prove of help.

Breed	Position		
	1970	1971	1972
Alsatians	1	1	1
Labrador Retrievers	2	2	2
Yorkshire Terriers	3	3	3
Cocker Spaniels	5	4	4
Toy Poodles	4	5	5
Rough Collies	6	6	6
Shetland Sheepdogs	7	7	8
Golden Retrievers	9	8	7
Miniature Poodles	8	9	10
West Highland White Terriers	10	10	12
Pekingese	11	11	11
Irish Setters	16	12	9
Boxers	12	13	15
Afghan Hounds	20	14	14
Cavalier King Charles Spaniels	17	15	13
English Springer Spaniel	18	21	16
Cairn Terriers	14	17	17
Pembroke Welsh Corgis	13	18	19
Old English Sheepdogs	24	19	18
Basset Hounds	23	20	20

A summary of the above indicates that while most of our breeds remain steady, Miniature Poodles and Corgis are drifting away from the top while Afghans and Irish Setters are bounding towards it. Use the information how you will, but please don't let it influence you too much either way. Choosing a fireside companion for a twelve-year span is a serious thing. Not only hasty marriages provide the opportunity for leisurely repentance!

The Royal Air Force is offered by their owners several thousand young Alsatians every year free of charge. This is neither patriotism nor generosity. It's an easy way of solving the problem of a dog which had grown much bigger, more boisterous and hungrier than when short-sighted people bought cuddly little pups. The moral is clear. But let's go on. Personally, I would like to own a Labrador but I doubt if a Labrador would like to own me because I spend half my time writing and the other half travelling by car which would bore it to distraction. You might have a yen for a couple of Irish Wolfhounds but if you live in a small house and have a limited budget, subdue it, because apart from space they cost pounds a week each to feed.

Many people like terriers but their alert, active high spirits do not suit everybody and particularly those who think their mother's staid Pug was the perfect pet. The hearty, outdoor types with rambling houses should choose gundogs; flat-bound stay-at-homes the 'toy' breeds, most of which are content to take their exercise pottering around the house and garden. If you are short of time, why follow fashion with a Poodle which needs a couple of hours' grooming every week when a Whippet's toilet only takes as many minutes? Why pick a Chihuahua to do a Bull Terrier's guard job? Why expect a Pyrenean Mountain Dog to make a good lap dog? In reality your choice boils down to a simple formula. The code word is 'stamp'. Or to be more precise S.T.A.M.P.: S = Space, T = Time, A = Activities, M = Money, P = Place of abode.

Looking at these in detail, the amount of space we have dictates the type of dog to which we can give a happy life. Great Danes and small houses for example do not, in my opinion, go together. Neither for that matter do Saint Bernards and fourth-floor flats. This may seem too obvious to state but it is often forgotten.

Time is important because large, active dogs require more exercise than small and inactive ones. Equally it takes ten or more times as long to groom an Old English Sheepdog adequately as it would to polish a Labrador.

The 'A' for activities refers to your own. Another way of describing this consideration would be by using the word 'inclinations'. Thus if you like walking for miles over the downs, accept the fact that a Pekingese would not be the ideal companion for you. On the other hand if you count a nightly walk to the post office, pillar box or public house as more than ample exercise, then you could easily fail to come to terms with a Dalmatian. This energetic dog will trot behind a horse for twenty miles and then ask 'When are we going for a walk?'

'M' stands for money, in the opinion of some a sordid subject which should not be allowed to enter into the pure relationship enjoyed between man and dog. What an absurd idea! Taken at its simplest, an Old English Mastiff will cost roughly six times as much to feed as a Pomeranian. Why undertake the feeding of the larger if your pocket is only able to cope satisfactorily with the smaller?

Finally 'P' is for place of residence. Briefly we should consider whether a country dog such as an English Springer Spaniel, a Labrador or a Greyhound could settle and relax in a flat in the centre of a big city. Conversely could some of the smaller breeds flower and feel their best in a bleak, remote and spartan area of the countryside?

A look at the six groups of dogs gives us the opportunity of making a reasonable and careful choice. Very often the same characteristics run right through a group. As examples can be mentioned the benevolence of the gundogs and the exuberance of terriers. I therefore devote the rest of this chapter to giving some indication of group background, together with further information respecting the most popular breeds in the respective groups.

Terrier Group

Almost without exception these are high-spirited and active dogs. Most of them have a working and country background but even so they have settled well in towns and built-up areas. Indeed it is from these districts that they obtain most of their support. They all need reasonable exercise but none demand that it should be excessive.

While it is not true that all terriers are bad tempered it must be admitted that the majority of them will not lightly suffer provocation from another dog. They are not then, in the true sense, 'old ladies' dogs' although it is a fact that many elderly ladies do own them and seem vastly satisfied with this arrangement.

AIREDALE: The king of terriers, produced about a hundred years ago by crossing local terriers with Otterhounds. At one time widely used for police work.

Despite their great size they are true terriers, and patient with children. High spirited but good guards.

BULL TERRIER: Originally bred to fight by crossing Bulldogs and White English Terriers.

Hard, strong, heavy and very muscular dogs. Full of fire but amenable to discipline, preferably by a man.

CAIRN TERRIER: One of the smallest, shaggiest and most popular terriers. Coat should not be stripped.

Although they only weigh 14 lb they are game but not aggressive. Very suitable for town houses and flats.

FOX TERRIER: Both Smooth and Wire-haired were originally bred for hunting. They have lively minds and bodies. Are good companions for children but will not tolerate boredom.

Smooths need little attention, but expert trimming is necessary to keep the Wires smart.

SEALYHAM TERRIER: A sporting dog bred by Captain Edwardes of Sealyham House, Haverfordwest, to dig otters and badgers.

Strong, robust, short-legged dogs whose once pugnacious temperament has been considerably subdued.

WEST HIGHLAND WHITE TERRIER: Smart, attractive, good tempered dogs of reasonable size for modern houses. Very adaptable, not aggressive and despite colour easy to keep clean.

Hound Group

This is subdivided into the hunting hounds, those that hunt by scent, and the coursing hounds, which are those that hunt by sight. For example, the Afghan, Borzoi and Whippet are obvious coursing hounds because, like the Greyhound they are built on fast and racy lines. When they see their quarry they hardly bother to use their nose because they can run so much faster than they can smell. Clearly then, these animals will never be happy unless they can occasionally indulge in their favourite pastime of galloping.

Hunting hounds include the Basset, the Beagle and the Dachshund, all of whom enjoy following a trail which means that it is very much easier to give them adequate exercise.

AFGHAN HOUND: An ancient breed only brought here about sixty years ago. Quiet, dignified but very active hounds which require space for exercise and time for daily grooming.

BASENJI: Barkless dogs from Central Africa brought to Britain in 1930. About the same size as a Fox Terrier. Very clean indoors. Need early and consistent training.

BASSET HOUND: Far bigger dogs than they look. Despite short legs often weigh upwards of 50 lb. Have appetites to match! Strong and need adequate, supervised exercise. Clearly unsuitable for small town houses.

BEAGLE: A good breed for frustrated Basset owners! Being miniature Foxhounds, they like exercise but given this can be happy anywhere.

DACHSHUND: There are six varieties in all. That is Smooth, Wire-haired and Long-haired, each in either Standard or Miniature size. Being small they are excellent town pets despite hunting background. Tendency to overweight must be watched.

WHIPPET: A miniature Greyhound. Neat, clean and elegant. Never aggressive. Happy anywhere.

Gundog Group

Without exception friendly, good natured, long suffering and trainable. All, however, have both a working and a country background which makes them ideal for country-dwellers who like a fair amount of exercise.

COCKER SPANIEL: Essentially a working dog used for rough shooting, hence the small, compact, robust body. They love the countryside and love working in it. Cheerful, good tempered, busy little dogs. Need bi-annual trimming.

ENGLISH SPRINGER: Twice the weight and size of the Cocker and even more determined to work. Trainable but definitely better suited to hedgerows than pavements.

GOLDEN RETRIEVER: Big, friendly dogs, suitable as retrievers, guards, guide dogs or companions. A good choice where families are young. Need space and exercise but do not seem to pine for the countryside.

IRISH SETTER: Attractive, stylish, fast moving, volatile animals,

A pointer in the field

at their happiest when ranging freely over wide moors. Sensitive, intelligent and easily trained.

LABRADOR RETRIEVER: Britain's top gundog. The ideal dog for countless families. Gentle, dependable, trainable and kind. The only possible disadvantages are his size and appetite. Has excelled at every task given him.

Toy Group

These spring from ancestors whose role in life has always been that of pet dog. They are, as the name implies, small and although not necessarily cheap to buy, certainly less costly to keep. Moreover the exercising problem is quite naturally much less acute than with large, active dogs because most toys can get all the exercise they need by running round the house and garden with their owners.

CHIHUAHUA: The world's smallest but not lacking self importance! Coat may be either smooth or long. Not over-keen on cold, rain or exercise! Very easy to house and feed.

CAVALIER KING CHARLES SPANIEL: A diminutive spaniel known in England for centuries. Good natured, elegant dogs with attractive colouring. Bigger than most toys at about 15 lb.

GRIFFON BRUXELLOIS: Bigger than the Chihuahua and usually more robust. Can also be smooth or rough coated. Very determined, independent little characters with big personalities.

PEKINGESE: During their hundred odd years in Britain they have established themselves as ever popular 'toys'. Long coated, glamorous, usually surprisingly willing to take exercise, they are sometimes stubborn but invariably good tempered.

PUG: Possibly the sturdiest 'toy'. Either black or fawn. Very fashionable in the past, now becoming popular again. Surprisingly active 'quicksilver' dogs.

YORKSHIRE TERRIER: Very small, attractive dogs with long, dark blue and rich tan coats. Excellent, lively companions. Coat needs considerable attention if to remain in perfect show condition.

Working Group

This consists of dogs which have served man over the centuries. Guard dogs, police dogs, guides, shepherds, drovers, even pullers of sledges. The implication is clear. Without exception these are active dogs with active minds. Unless exercised physically and mentally they are unlikely to be completely happy.

ALSATIAN *(German Shepherd Dog)*: Britain's top dog. Probably the world's top dog. And certainly the top dog for work of every description. Properly housed, fed, trained and handled they are unbeatable. They are not suitable, however, for small houses, shallow pockets, the aged or the idle!

BOXER: Another German dog with a background of work. Even so is rarely aggressive and particularly suitable for young boys. Is very strong, boisterous and slow to mature. Needs space indoors and out.

COLLIE (ROUGH): Beautiful dogs with expressive heads. Almost never worked now. Intelligent and sensitive. Very trainable. Coat needs reasonable attention.

CORGI: Small, pert, rather 'bossy' dogs which are worked in Wales for herding sheep and cattle. Not always ideal with young children. Very trainable. Easy to feed and are hardy and robust.

DOBERMANN: Keen, hard dogs, used in the same way as Alsatians. Need firm but just training. Very active and powerful. Not cut out for an idle existence.

GREAT DANE: Huge, benevolent dogs with charming manners. Never aggressive but size is a distinct 'deterrent'. Big eaters and expensive to rear. Need plenty of space.

OLD ENGLISH SHEEPDOG: An ancient breed originally used to drive sheep and cattle to market but recently given an enormous popularity boost by the well-known paint advertisements plus well-known owners such as the Beatles and the late Bobby Kennedy. A striking and powerful dog, slow to mature and settle. Reasonably placid with maturity but coat needs constant work.

SHETLAND SHEEPDOG: Miniature Collies. Very sensitive and trainable. Importance of getting one with the right temperament – that is not timid – cannot be over-stressed. Coat needs moderate attention.

Utility Group

This is really a collection of breeds which do not fit naturally elsewhere! There is a wide range of size and temperament. For example Poodles, Dalmatians, Chows and French Bulldogs have little in common. Each then must be considered by a potential owner on their individual breed characteristics.

BOSTON TERRIER: Strong though small, determined but not aggressive, smart but easily groomed, this breed has many advantages for those who like the unusual. Modest in their demand for space, exercise and food.

BULLDOG: The national breed. Despite terrifying appearance

they are particularly good natured. Although not over keen on exercise or hot weather can be very active on occasions.

DALMATIAN: Came from the stables and cannot have too much exercise. Tendency to moult which is inconvenient. Very smart and distinctive. Good natured.

POODLE: They come in three sizes and hardly need introduction. The Standards usually around 22 inches at the shoulder, the Miniatures under 15 inches and the Toys under 11 inches. All are intelligent, trainable and good tempered. They never moult but their coats need regular and costly attention.

If you are interested in one of the seventy odd breeds not mentioned above (a full list will be found in Appendix 'A') by all means consider that. Then make a list of every breed which appeals to you. Harden your heart and delete every one which is clearly unsuitable. You will be left with maybe three or four which could fit in with life as you must, or choose to live it.

Now away with caution and away with advice. Pick the one you like best. A dog is a very personal possession.

4 | Choice of a Puppy

At this point, and presuming you have decided to follow the advice given in the previous chapter, you are all set to be a successful dog owner.

But oddly enough, many people who have reached this stage by the exercise of reason go on to make a serious mistake. Having chosen their breed by logic they let emotion take over when they buy the puppy. This chapter is designed to help you avoid the same trap. Designed to steel your brain before an unsuitable puppy steals your heart. Designed to persuade you that there is nothing cold-blooded about making a calculated choice and nothing to be ashamed of in choosing a puppy with the same insistence upon rejecting the unsuitable as there would be in resisting the temptation to buy a second rate washing machine.

But even before you reach this stage, you must decide the simple question of whether you want a dog or a bitch. Since they are born in roughly equal numbers there is little risk that the sex of your choice will not be available. And since the people who prefer one or the other are also born in roughly equal quantities, there is no risk that all puppies of the sex you decide against will be for ever left upon the breeder's shelf.

In many ways the choice is a matter of personal preference. I have owned many dogs but always feel myself drawn closer to the bitches in my life. Many with equal, perhaps greater experience, feel the exact reverse. If you do not already have a preference, the following facts may help.

The bitch normally comes into season for the first time at around eight months of age and thereafter at intervals of approximately six months for the remainder of her life. During these periods of season there is a slight discharge and she emits a faint scent undetectable to human beings but highly attractive to male dogs. At this time she has a strong, even primitive desire to mate and, since the aforementioned scent will have attracted suitors, there will be ample opportunity to do so if you relax your guard.

In effect this means that during the two to three weeks at a time when the urge is upon her she must remain within your sight at all times. Shutting her in the garden is useless. She may not be able to jump out but males can, and will, jump in. Similarly when taken for a walk her previous good manners and obedience can no longer be taken for granted. Her deep instincts may cause her first to wander then to run away from you. She is only safe on a lead.

When not in season she is virtually sex-less. No male has any attraction for her and she tends to concentrate all of her affection upon her owners. This makes her biddable and trainable. She has no distractions and her only desire is to share her life with you and please.

The dog has no cycle as inconvenient as that of the bitch. Additionally any mistake he might commit will not land his owners with a litter of unwanted mongrel puppies! But although the dog has no time of peak interest in sex it must be admitted that he is at all times interested in, sometimes even distracted by the subject. This may be regrettable but it is natural. One of his primary instincts in life must be to reproduce himself. The other is to be your friend and companion. Sometimes the two can be reconciled, and usually they are. So we finish where we began in that both sexes have minor disadvantages and it is up to you to decide which, if either, you prefer to live with.

The decision taken, there are three sources from which you can buy your puppy. First there is a friend, relation or some other private individual. Next there is a pet shop or livestock dealer. Finally there is the breeding kennel which specializes in the breed of your choice.

The author has no hesitation in recommending a recognized breeding kennel. Breeding livestock is only one of the many pastimes at which a professional has the edge on an amateur. The friend from whom you buy a puppy may or may not know very much about rearing and irreparable damage could have been done to the puppy's constitution during the first and formative weeks. Additionally, a number of well-meaning amateurs who breed from 'Susie' seem to imagine that because she is likeable and indeed well liked, she will throw puppies which are automatically more valuable than those 'ordinary' dogs from a kennel! In fact the kennel dog is much more likely to be better bred and better reared, if only because professionals cannot afford the luxury of second rate propositions.

Pet shops and dog dealers are also of course professionals and as such they try to do their best to preserve their reputations. Alas this is not always easy because one of the hazards of their trade is that they are middle men without allegiance to either the producer or the consumer. They buy the pups as well as they can and try to get the best stock possible at a price which will show them a reasonable margin of profit. Nothing blameworthy about that but it is almost certainly not an ideal way of getting a living animal from the side of its mother to its place by a family hearth because there's a gap, a no man's land, in the vital centre.

Recognized and reputable breeding kennels have the advantage of being able to look after the puppies from birth. In the majority of cases they have done them well and become very attached to them. This, however, does not mean that no questions need be asked. The man who shops for a young dog without making a thorough investigation is likely to buy a pup in more senses than one!

Above all, the buyer should satisfy himself that the chosen pup is healthy. Ideally one should always take a veterinary surgeon to the kennels when choosing. However, this is not always possible and would, in any case, add considerably to the cost. While it is not possible for the layman to be certain, there are numerous warning signals which the customer ignores at his peril.

We should therefore regard with particular suspicion, runny noses, runny eyes and diarrhoea, all of which are indications of ill health, possibly of a serious nature. At the same time one should look on the stomach for spots which can indicate incipient distemper, for red and spongy gums which could mean other problems and for inflamed, sore or smelly ears, all of which are clear indications of bad kennel management, if nothing worse.

Although you are buying a puppy and not the establishment, it is still a good idea to look at the general cleanliness of the kennel and the runs. You may also have the opportunity of looking at the parents or at least the mother. Clearly, having just bred a litter she will not be in perfect show condition but she should have a clean, fresh and healthy look about her. Only when you have completely satisfied yourself on this vital score of health should you consider a purchase.

Next you should pay the greatest attention to the temperament of the puppy because you are going to live with it for a long time. The two major faults of temperament are aggression and timidity. The former would never be apparent in one so young. Timidity, however, often shows at an early age and the puppy to avoid is the one that cringes when you touch it or even worse hides away and refuses to let you do so. In contrast the one you should take to your heart is the bold one which takes you to his!

What, in my opinion, pet owners should not do when buying a pedigree dog is worry about the so-called 'points'. If you want a pet Dalmatian what does it matter to you if its spots are a shade too close? If a Poodle's head is a little broad, a Collie's rather short or a Yorkshire Terrier's ears on the big side? Of course if you want a show specimen these and similar points are vital. You will seek perfection on all breed points and incidentally have to reconcile yourself to paying a small fortune to get them!

But you don't. You want a pet dog – a family dog. Certainly one which is recognizable and an agreeable looking representative of its breed but also one which above all is fit, cheerful and easy going enough to share your life. Temperament, for the pet owner, is all.

Age has some bearing on this, something which the breeder has always known instinctively. In any case practical economics encourages them to sell puppies when they are seven or eight weeks old because of the rapidly escalating food bills. Puppy buyers welcome this because they always want their youngsters while they are young, pretty and amusing. But recently a psychologist from Washington University has been studying the position from the dog's point of view. And unlike most psychologists he has decided that we have been doing the right thing all the time!

He traced the pups' thought process from birth onwards. For the first three weeks they are virtually vegetables. Then occurs a sudden change. They begin to bark, wag their tails and react to humans. In other words they become individuals. If at this age they are taken from the litter they become too dependent on people. Maybe they think they are humans themselves. Anyway they become anti-social to other dogs and stay that way.

In contrast, puppies left with the litter from four to twelve weeks of age and with *no* human contact, react the other way. They become wild and uneasy in the presence of humans. They prefer the company of other dogs and frequently make poor house pets. So obviously you aim to take delivery of puppies somewhere between these two extremes. Six to ten weeks is considered ideal. At this age the pup will have had active experience of living with other dogs but still be able to adjust to living with people. From then on, forming the dog's character is up to the owner. The pup is receptive to good or bad influences. In other words being impressionable, it can be made or marred.

Puppy being inoculated

Now come a few small administrative details which it is well worth attending to at this point if only because many kennel owners are so busy and pre-occupied with running the kennels that they are not particularly good correspondents! Before you pay your money and go, ask for a pedigree form and ascertain whether the puppy has been registered with the Kennel Club. If it has, obtain a signed transfer form so that you can re-register it in your own name.

It is also worth finding out whether the pup has been wormed and inoculated. Although there is no real objection to worming twice, to repeat inoculation would be an unnecessary expense. Finally, ask for a diet sheet so that you do not make too abrupt a change in the regime at the same time as you are already introducing sufficient upset by changing the pup's home.

5 | Settling In

A puppy leaving its mother and entering a family home for the first time is charming but totally uncivilized. And that, if it were capable of formulating thoughts is exactly what it would say about you!

The point is that your thought processes are totally different. You start off miles apart and it is almost incredible that in a few weeks you will be close together. The pup will of course have had to make most of the adjustments and since even the most bigoted would admit we are more intelligent than dogs, that is no bad thing. Somehow, in a few brief weeks we have to mould this little character to our lives, our habits, our customs and our standard of values.

Since most of us are determined not to have the house turned into an inside toilet, we usually face the first problem within minutes of putting a newly bought pup on the floor. House training, whether we like it or not, becomes a priority task.

Mercifully with most pups it does not take long if the owner or trainer is consistent and even tempered. A week is enough for some pups, perhaps a fortnight or more for others. The trick is to use brain and not brawn.

Never resort to smacking, beating, shouting or that humiliating business of rubbing the puppy's nose in any mess it has made. The point to remember with puppies is that when they first wake up, and soon after they have eaten or drunk, they cannot help relieving themselves. Your job for the first few days, and it is a full time job, is to pop the puppy outside a few seconds before it happens. In this way you soon bring about an association of ideas so that the puppy recognizes the place you have selected, and obliges you instantly.

Every mistake made in the house should be looked upon as your mistake rather than the puppy's, and if you watch the young dog at all hours for the first few days, you will not have to break the puppy of being dirty indoors as well as training it to go outside.

During the night you must expect puddles from young puppies because until they are four or five months old they are incapable of holding out for very long. From this it follows that the time should be cut down as much as possible by putting them out last thing at night and the first thing in the morning. First thing means just that.

If you let the puppy hear you walking about upstairs while you dress, most certainly an accident will occur. You should put on a dressing gown, walk downstairs and put the puppy out even before you pat him and say 'Good morning'. Delays produce puddles and puddles produce more puddles! The dog is a creature of habit and you may decide whether you take advantage of this or suffer because of it.

There is a school of thought which believes in allowing puppies to use indoor litter trays for the first few weeks in their new home. I do not share this view. To teach a puppy a trick is difficult enough but to un-teach one is more difficult. Having spent a few weeks teaching a pup it is cute to wet on a tray in the corner of the kitchen, you have to start teaching it all over again that it is not cute. And as if this was not enough at this same time you start teaching it that it *is* cute to go to a selected spot in the garden.

Little wonder that the poor dog's brain reels. Little wonder that the owner's does the same until both wonder whether they have bitten off more than they can chew.

Which emotive words lead to another problem which must be faced fairly early. The instinct of pups to chew shoes, carpets, table legs, trousers or fingers. It's all the same to them. Leave them to their own devices and in no time at all you will probably have no clothes, legs or furniture at all!

The simple answer is to provide chewable toys at the beginning such as whalehide twists, old slippers and large bones. And then forbid all chewing of any other objects. At the first little nibble, rap out the word 'No' – and mean it. Even if your pup does not speak English, he will know what 'No' means if you use the right tone of voice.

So already you are embarking on a training career and whether he likes it or not the pup is on the way to becoming a pupil. He has many more lessons to learn and if at this stage you begin to feel sorry for the poor little chap, remember that in the long run it's all for his own good. Dogs are very like us in that they would prefer to be liked rather than disliked. It's fun to be popular and a well-behaved dog is likely to be just that. Conversely one which is bad mannered can be a sore trial, particularly when he is met at a friend's house.

1   The Dog in the Family!

2a   A Guide Dog for the Blind

2b   Police dog trained for drug detection

3a   Police dogs in training

3b   Alpine rescue dog at work in Norway

4a Mr. Wallace with his demonstration team of Border Collies used at Sheepdog
    trials

4b Teaching the 'sit' and 'stay'

5   Alsatian (German Shepherd Dog). The top dog for work of every description

6   Golden Retriever. Big friendly dog, suitable as retriever, guide dog or companion

7   Rough Collie. Intelligent, sensitive and very trainable

8   Standard Poodle puppies. Largest of the three Poodles, standing up to 24 inches at the shoulder

The two most hazardous pastimes I know are criticizing people's children and criticizing people's dogs. Both are guaranteed to bring a beautiful friendship to an abrupt end. The pity of it is that so many unendurable canine bad manners such as trouser pulling, barking, lap sitting and white-hairs-on-suit shedding have been deliberately taught to young pups.

To avoid falling into the same trap yourself remember that if you teach your dog to bark in the house you may well regret it. That jumping up to welcome mistress is quite cute when the pup is young and clean but exasperating when his feet are muddy. Jumping on chairs and beds is another trick which loses its appeal with the passage of time and second thoughts on the subject are even more hastily arrived at if the dog is white and given to moulting.

Why teach a young dog that it's amusing to pull at your clothing? Why teach him that making a nuisance of himself at the table brings a rewarding titbit? That he can play with and destroy your slippers? That it's clever to chase cats? That strangers may be growled at?

In short, why teach him that any bad manners are engaging? The most popular dogs, like the most popular children, are the well behaved ones and this quality is not second nature. It has to be taught.

Another problem to be faced right away is where the pup shall sleep. And I come down firmly with the suggestion that a house dog's place is in the house.

While kennel dogs, particularly those kept in large numbers, live happily in outside kennels, a single dog cannot be healthy or happy in even the most luxurious kennel. A family dog only flourishes when it shares the family life.

Some people think that a dog may be a better guard if kept outside. This is not so because except on rare sites, dogs which live outside must be fastened in some way, either by confinement or by a chain. This means that they are prevented from guarding the house even if they wished to do so. When they are kept indoors however, they are in a position to keep out unwelcome callers and perhaps even more important, to give the alarm should anybody approach.

Even indoors, however, a dog should have a bed of his own

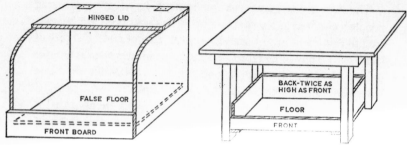

Home-made dog beds

because it gives him a retreat and you more useable floor space.
It should be raised, say, four inches from the floor to avoid
draughts. It should have a back and sides for the same purpose and
be lined with something comfortable. A handyman can easily
make this bed. Alternatively it can be constructed on similar
lines using the four legs of the kitchen table as side supports and
nailing hardboard on to them. The importance of raising the
floor by four inches still applies.

Alternatively beds, boxes or baskets can be bought from any
pet shop. Baskets are frequently the most decorative and also the
cheapest to buy but they do have the curious disadvantage of
encouraging even reasonable dogs into the chewing habit!

Although the problem of formal exercise will not crop up for a while, most new pup owners waste little time in buying a collar and lead at this point and nothing I can do will dissuade them. I therefore merely advise that you buy cheap ones because he will grow out of them long before they have had any real use.

There is always the temptation to buy a harness instead of a collar, and particularly for the small or toy breeds, this is unwise. A harness does have the unfortunate effect of encouraging puppies to pull on the lead because they can put their body weight behind the project.

Few puppies care to pull with their necks but a harness turns them all into cart horses! Apart from the inconvenience of this habit, it often has the effect of distorting the bones in their shoulders and fore legs during the formative months.

Coats are normally not necessary for dogs. They have excellent and waterproof coats of their own. Exceptions might be made for the very small, light coated breeds which feel the cold, such as Italian Greyhounds or Chihuahuas. Very adverse weather conditions, that is temperatures well below freezing, might also warrant the wearing of coats, although even then it is not normally necessary.

Wet weather never demands that a coat be worn. All a coat in rain does is collect water and hold it close to the dog's body. He cannot even shake it dry as he would his own coat. If you must keep your dog dry, buy him a waterproof or mackintosh.

He will of course need water to drink and when you buy the dog you should also buy a water bowl and vow that throughout his lifetime, fresh clean water will always be available. For the first few days the pup will probably drink too much. The novelty of having free 'food' permanently available will amuse him. But this stage will pass quickly and he will then drink only as and when he needs it.

Before coming to the important question of feeding puppies during the first few months in the home, a warning: you will almost certainly have to face an immediate show down on the sleeping arrangements. No matter how comfortable the bed you have provided, the pup will most certainly be very unwilling to stay in it on the first night. Before being too harshly critical we should remember that he has never been alone in this world before. He has always had either his mother or his litter mates to keep him warm and to give him that vital comfort and companionship.

As you bid him goodnight and walk out of the kitchen to go to bed, he will howl. You have a problem on your hands and the only question is whether to fight the battle this first night or to put it off until his new habit is that of sleeping with you. The longer you put it off the less is the possibility of you winning. The advice is given, therefore, that you harden your heart and keep on walking. If you make the mistake of giving in to his crying, of coming down to soothe him, even to scold him, being a ready pupil he will learn quickly and perform the same trick again.

It is sometimes recommended that you leave new puppies with a stone hot water bottle under their blanket because this gives them not only warmth, which they can probably do without in the average heated house, but a certain feeling of security. I would not argue with this. Some even advocate that an old alarm clock be left under the blankets, because the ticking gives evidence of some sort of life. The author has never taken this advice – and that for the simple reason that he has yet to own a puppy which did not have the enthusiastic inquisitiveness to find and dismember the unfortunate clock in a matter of moments!

And so to the most important part of this chapter, that is the 'inner dog'! There is no chance of forgetting it because the pup will remind you very soon after you get him home.

The full subject of feeding dogs is discussed in Chapter 7 of this book and it is suggested that you read it at your leisure if only because it may dispel a few widely held misconceptions. But with a hungry pup whining at your feet there is insufficient time to consider principles. If you have been given a supply of the pup's usual food by the breeder, give it to him without delay. It might even be wise to carry on with his usual diet for say forty-eight hours to avoid additional upsets.

Even so, you should realize that some diets suggested by breeders are unnecessarily complicated. Feeding puppies can be simplified provided the following basic rules are observed:

1. Feed a balanced diet containing approximately equal amounts by weight of (dry) cereal and protein foods.

2. Give two main meals a day, morning and evening.
3. Feed to appetite; if the puppy cleans up the dish and is obviously not satisfied, give more. A healthy puppy usually eats its fill in less than five minutes.
4. Give milk daily up to the age of six months: from ¼ pint/day for small breeds up to 1 pint/day for Alsatians.

Owing to the variation in size and rate of growth already referred to, it is impossible to state precise quantities of food for puppies. The feeding chart at the end of this chapter *must be treated only as a guide*. It suggests diets for the three breeds discussed under weaning (Chapter 12), and thus covers dogs ranging in adult weight from about 15 to 65 lb. Note that the morning meal is gradually increased in size while the evening food remains almost constant so that the adult dog receives virtually one main meal a day. There is no objection to the alternative procedure of increasing the evening meal. This is entirely a matter of the owner's convenience, provided that the chosen regime is adhered to.

Nearly all healthy puppies have appetites to match and there should be no problems over refusal. Nor is there any need to vary the food if a balanced diet is being given: the dog is a creature of habit. Many owners, especially of toy dogs, make the mistake of expecting the puppy to eat too much and tempting him with special delicacies. The usual result is a fat, finickety feeder.

Supplements are not normally necessary as most established proprietary dog foods, dry or tinned, are already fortified with vitamins and minerals. This applies to diets composed of dog meal, tinned meat and milk. If, however, fresh minced meat and a plain cereal are preferred as a basis, it is essential to give the nutrients which are deficient in such a diet. These are the vitamins A and D and the minerals calcium, phosphorus and magnesium. In natural surroundings, the vitamins are probably provided by liver and the minerals by bones, and these are the preferred sources for the pet puppy. Give liver in place of half the minced meat once a week and provide a cooked marrow bone for the puppy to gnaw. This supplies minerals and keeps the teeth in excellent condition. Never give chicken, rabbit, fish and other splintery bones which may lodge in the throat or perforate the intestines. As alternatives cod liver oil will provide the vitamins, and sterilized bone flour, or a proprietary supplement, the minerals, but be careful to control the quantities in accordance with the maker's instructions.

Puppy Feeding Chart

BREED	AGE	WEIGHT lb	MORNING MEAL	MIDDAY MEAL	EVENING MEAL
Miniature Poodle	8 weeks	4	1½ oz puppy meal / 2 oz milk	2 oz milk	1 oz puppy meal / 2 oz milk
	3 months	6	2 oz puppy meal / 1 oz meat	3 oz milk	1 oz puppy meal / 2 oz milk
	4 months	8	3 oz puppy meal / 2 oz meat	—	2 small dog biscuits / 4 oz milk
	6 months	12	4 oz puppy meal / 3 oz meat	—	3 biscuits / 4 oz milk
	9 months	14	3 oz dog meal / 4 oz meat	—	4 biscuits
Beagle	8 weeks	8	3 oz puppy meal / 3 oz milk	4 oz milk	3 oz puppy meal / 3 oz milk
	3 months	12	4 oz puppy meal / 2 oz meat	5 oz milk	3 oz puppy meal / 5 oz milk
	4 months	17	6 oz puppy meal / 4 oz meat	—	5 small dog biscuits / 10 oz milk
	6 months	25	9 oz puppy meal / 6 oz meat	—	5 biscuits / 10 oz milk
	9 months	30	6 oz dog meal / 6 oz meat	—	5 biscuits

BREED	AGE	WEIGHT lb	MORNING MEAL	MIDDAY MEAL	EVENING MEAL
Labrador Retriever	8 weeks	12	4 oz puppy meal 5 oz milk	10 oz milk	4 oz puppy meal 5 oz milk
	3 months	20	8 oz puppy meal 3 oz meat	10 oz milk	4 oz puppy meal 10 oz milk
	4 months	30	12 oz puppy meal 6 oz meat	10 oz milk	4 oz puppy meal 10 oz milk
	6 months	50	16 oz puppy meal 12 oz meat	—	10 small dog biscuits 10 oz milk
	9 months	60	10 oz dog meal 12 oz meat	—	10 biscuits

6 | Care and Grooming

All dogs need some sort of maintenance. This need not be a full-time occupation, but you can make it one if you wish. Most of us don't. So we buy the right tools to save time and then decide to do the small things that are required at regular intervals rather than compensate for days or weeks of neglect by long, exasperating and boring sessions.

The maintenance, which could be lumped together under the all embracing title of grooming consists in fact of attention to coat, ears, eyes, teeth and nails.

Maybe we should start by considering bathing. To be more precise, in deciding whether bathing, a tedious chore, is even necessary. And in my opinion it is not. It often does more harm than good and in the long run, that is if practised regularly, it undoubtedly softens the coat which is the reverse of what nature intended and common sense demands. But of this more later. First I will deal with the preferable alternative which is daily brushing.

Grooming

You will hardly need to be told that whatever method of grooming you decide upon, the amount of time you will have to devote to it will depend upon the breed you have chosen. A very large breed will take ten times as long to do merely because there's ten times as much of it. An Afghan will take ten times as long as a Greyhound to brush merely because it has ten times as much hair.

Probably the breed which demands the most work is the Old English Sheepdog because it has the most coat and bulk. Some owners of Standard Poodles and Afghans might contest this. But perhaps not too seriously.

Few would contest that the dog I own myself requires the least. It is a Griffon weighing about 5 lb and it has a short, smooth coat. If I had to groom it, ten minutes a day would be ample. In fact the cat took over the task as the pup walked in the door five years ago and has been at it ever since!

Let us leave aside such exceptional good fortune and accept that the time, and the tools needed for adequate grooming depend largely on the breed of dog you have chosen. Briefly, however, we can divide them into heavy-coated breeds such as Old English Sheepdogs, Poodles, Pekingese, etc.; medium-coated dogs – that

ng-coated dog
ng combed

is Cocker Spaniels and Shetland Sheepdogs; and smooth-coated breeds such as Whippets and Boxers.

For the heavy-coated breeds you will want a brush with nylon bristles set in a rubber pad. This should be used daily, brushing the dog from the tail to the top of the head and taking special care to brush down to the roots. A superficial top brushing serves no practical purpose – indeed it often succeeds in matting the coat. Particular attention must be paid to those places where matts and tangles form, such as round the hindquarters and under what might be called the 'armpits'. If any tangles are found they must be teased out gently by hand, although in bad cases it may be necessary to cut them away even though this leaves an unsightly mark. After a thorough brushing, a wide-toothed steel comb should be passed through the coat to ensure that it is quite free of tangles.

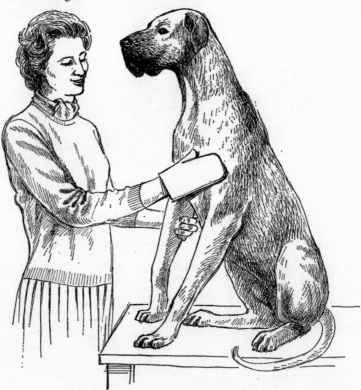

Short-coated dog being groomed with a hound glove

To fall into the temptation of using the comb first – that is before the brush – is a mistake because it encourages you to tug at the matts, much to the dog's discomfort. It also breaks his coat and removes so much hair that it will soon appear thin and lacking in bloom.

During the brushing operation the dog should be encouraged from puppyhood to lie on his side with his feet towards you for the grooming session. Relaxation is encouraged by gentleness and tension is manufactured by clumsiness, harshness or bad temper. If you are in the mood where you have to do something or scream it's better just to scream. Or saw up some logs. You can't wait for ever for the grooming mood to sneak up on you but it's certainly smarter not to start if the nerves are already jangling!

With the medium-coated dogs you need the same tools and follow the same grooming procedure. Clearly it will not take so long nor prove so character testing! The easiest dogs to groom are of course the smooth-coated breeds because five minutes a day is ample. The best tool is a hound glove, that is a glove which has short bristles in the palm. A brief brushing or massage from nose to tail will suffice to keep the smooth-coated breeds clean, fresh and feeling fit.

Bathing

While bathing must be dealt with, it should be appreciated that as long as the brushing is systematically performed, bathing is virtually unnecessary, except in those rare cases where a dog gets particularly dirty through, for example, digging in the coal cellar or rolling in mess in the fields. Regular grooming keeps the coat clean right down to the skin and moreover it keeps it supple and glossy.

Bathing, regrettably, often has the reverse effect by drying out the skin and making the coat 'stare'. Moreover, it softens the hair on the dog and removes the natural oils which makes it inevitable that the new fluffy coat will pick up more dirt, making bathing more necessary in the future. Thus the more you bath the more you have to.

On the occasions when you do have to bath a dog, and incidentally your nose is a good guide in this connection, you should use a veterinary shampoo. A dog's skin is much more sensitive than our own and therefore most, if not all, of our toilet soaps, and particularly household soaps, are much too harsh. There are many special dog shampoos on the market and, as an equally satisfactory and cheaper alternative, consider the simple and unbranded green soft soap.

The dog should be stood in a sink, bath or suitable container and, before starting, his ears should be plugged with cotton wool. He should then be rinsed all over with clean water, after which the shampoo should be rubbed in, starting from the head but taking particular care to keep the soap out of his eyes. Work down his back and then down his legs to his feet. Afterwards, rinse thoroughly in clean, running water. Repeat the whole process and your dog is ready to dry. Something which he will be only too pleased to organize for himself if given the opportunity!

Carry him therefore to a place where you do not mind having a shower bath, put him on the ground and let him shake. He will get rid of half of the moisture in a matter of moments. After this dry him thoroughly with a rough towel and then take him for a short walk, preferably on a lead unless you want his natural instincts to roll in dirt to nullify your previous efforts. The modest exercise will produce sufficient body heat to dry off the remaining moistness. But before he is completely dry, you should first comb, then brush his coat in the way that you want it to grow. The shampoo and set is complete!

Ears

Ears are a very sore subject in more ways than one. Some dogs suffer from afflictions in the ear but an even greater number suffer from the well meaning attempts of owners to effect cures. In fact the troubles which afflict ears are legion and the sight of a dog shaking his head or rubbing his ears may mean they are inflamed, clogged with wax, infected by microbes or half a dozen other conditions, often loosely called 'canker'. To attempt to cure all these by putting in canker ointment or canker powder or spirit, is a mistake. Each separate condition requires separate treatment and the wrong one frequently does more harm than good by aggravating an already sensitive area. Apart then from cleaning out the part of the inside of the ear which you can see with a pad of cotton wool, moistened with olive oil, the treatment of ears is something best left to veterinary surgeons who can make a proper diagnosis and treat accordingly.

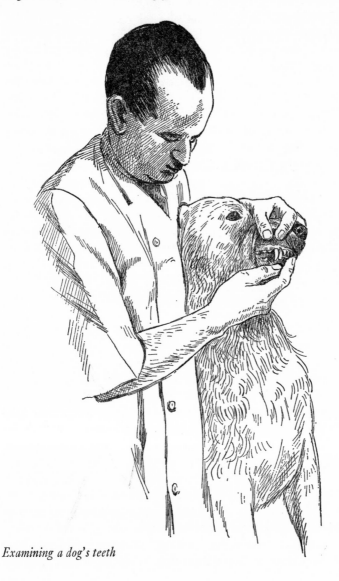

Examining a dog's teeth

Eyes

Fortunately, few pet owners interfere with a dog's eyes except in those cases where eyes water. The classic treatment here is bathing. Like so many other classic treatments, it is incorrect. Wet eyes are not in need of more water. Instead, moisten a pad of cotton wool in a solution of weak tea or milk, wring out thoroughly and wipe away the moisture. If done daily this should improve the condition and remove the unsightly marks left under the eyes.

Teeth

Teeth in a healthy dog require very little regular attention, although they should be examined occasionally. Bones have the effect of cleaning teeth and keeping them in good condition. Hard dog biscuits have a similar effect. In spite of these however, and particularly in the case of older dogs, some stains or tartar formations do appear. These can be scraped off by the pet's owner but it is a task better performed by a veterinary surgeon who is unlikely to chip or damage the enamel, or for that matter prod the gum.

Nose

At this point, we should perhaps mention the dog's nose because few people can avoid looking at this and reaching certain conclusions. Let it be said that while in general a cool, damp nose is a sign of health and a hot, dry one is the reverse, this rule is by no means reliable. An excessive discharge from the nose may be a symptom of distemper. On the other hand it may only be caused by a foreign body or a smoky atmosphere.

Nails

Now to the dog's nails which need treatment in accordance with the life the dog leads. A dog which is exercised on concrete, hard roads or pavements will usually wear his nails down himself and they will need no attention from you. Those, however, who walk only on carpeted floors, lawns and in the park, will have feet which tend to splay and nails which grow until they are hooked, unsightly and uncomfortable. They will then require to be shortened by cutting or filing. Filing is preferable because the click of cutters frightens some dogs. The file used should be a small 6-inch file of medium grade and care must be taken not to

Puppy's nails being filed

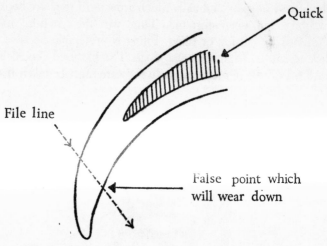

The right way to file a dog's nail

file into the 'quick' – that is the small, light coloured vein which can be seen when you hold the nail to the light.

Do not try to recover a year's neglect at one sitting. The front of the nail should be filed as illustrated which leaves a false point at the back which will wear down as the dog takes exercise. During this process the quick will retract allowing the same procedure to be followed at regular intervals until the nail is the required length.

Dew claws normally need no attention, principally because in most cases they have been removed soon after birth by the breeder or veterinary surgeon. Those that are left on sometimes catch in undergrowth or clothing and tear the skin. In cases like this, as they serve no useful purpose, the advice of a veterinary surgeon should be taken on the advisability of their removal.

Other requirements

Having dealt with brushes, combs, beds, nail files, etc., it might be as well to complete the list of things which have to be purchased at some time during the life of a dog. These consist of a lead, collar or harness, in certain cases a coat and, quite certainly, a veterinary thermometer. The latter is dealt with in Chapter 7

I   It's never too soon to learn

II   *Top left :* Labrador Retriever
      Above : Golden Retriever
      Left : Cocker Spaniel
      Bottom left : Irish Setter
      Below : Miniature Poodle

III *Above:* Shetland Sheepdog
Top right: Alsatian (G.S.D.)
Right: Rough Collie
Below: Yorkshire Terrier
Bottom right: Dalmatian

IVa West Highland White Terrier and puppy

IVb Telerecording a dog-biscuit commercial

of this book but it might be as well to make the point now that a thermometer is a most valuable aid to full health.

All dogs require a collar either separate or combined with a lead. The Control of Dogs Order (1930) requires that any dog on the public highway, must have his owner's name and address fastened to his collar. In the past it was customary to engrave this on a metal plaque which was fastened permanently to the collar. This system has some disadvantages, one of which is that while dogs grow until their collars are too small for them, there is the temptation to use it long after it has become too tight because it is engraved. Additionally, it is now fashionable to wear light-weight and thin collars. In this case, fashion is right because some of the heavy, old-fashioned collars must have been quite a burden.

The modern alternative to the engraved plaque is a disc or medallion such as those supplied by the Tail-Waggers' Club, Old Change House, Cannon Street, London EC4M 6XB, to all dogs which are enrolled as members. These medallions can of course be obtained elsewhere and suitably engraved but membership of the Tail-Waggers' Club is still worthwhile, not only because it still lives up to its original motto 'I help my pals' but because one day it might help you through the medium of its very excellent advisory service.

An alternative to the collar and separate lead is the modern type of lead and collar combined. These are made either of whale hide, plastic or nylon. They have a large loop at the end of the lead which slips over the dog's head and an attachment which enables it to be reduced in size after it has been put on.

Finally there is the harness, so often used on Toy dogs; in the writer's opinion, inadvisably. The disadvantages of a harness are many. In addition to the points already made on page 51, they tend to wear the coat in many places which spoils, for example, the mane of a Pekingese or a Chow. You will, in any case, need a collar and lead, as distinct from a harness when you come to train your dog so it is as well to accustom him to wearing one right from the start.

Coats are often worn by dogs (see page 51) – curiously enough generally in towns rather than the countryside; in other words in the place where they least need it. Rain harms few if any dogs, but this is not to say that they should be allowed to remain wet. Neither for that matter should they be given a bath when they come in from a storm. They are already wet enough! A chamois leather is extremely valuable however, because you can dry, massage and warm with it all at the same time.

7 | Feeding

A dog is fed every day, and if not fed correctly will deteriorate in health and condition. Therefore feeding is the most important single aspect of dog care with which the ordinary pet owner is concerned. The majority of owners realize their responsibilities and go to considerable expense and trouble to provide what they consider a suitable diet. Quite often, though less frequently than in the past, and in spite of this care, dogs are incorrectly fed.

There is a widely held misconception that a dog, being classed as a carnivore, must be fed almost exclusively meat. Meat is a valuable food but it is neither nutritionally complete nor essential. Whatever the primeval dog's feeding habits, the domestic dog of today thrives on omnivorous diets, very similar to those of man himself.

The secret of correct feeding is the balanced diet; food which provides all the essential nutrients in sufficient amounts, and in the correct proportions to one another, for the required purpose. In this case the purpose is the maintenance of sound health and physique in the adult dog.

What are these essential nutrients, how much of each does the dog need and in what types of food can they be found? Like men and other mammals the dog needs to obtain from his diet:

ENERGY
: supplied mainly by fats and carbohydrates.

BUILDING MATERIALS
: the water, protein, fat and minerals of which his body is composed.

VITAMINS
: organic chemicals needed in very small amounts as catalysts of numerous body processes.

1. Energy

Every activity uses up energy which can be obtained only by digestion of the food eaten, or breakdown of the body's own tissues. Even when asleep an animal needs energy to maintain body processes such as circulation of the blood. The energy value of food is measured in Calories. The calorie value of food varies according to its composition: water provides no energy, pure protein and carbohydrate can contribute about 1,800 calories per pound weight, but fats and edible oils are the richest source, yielding over 4,000 calories a pound.

Many factors influence a dog's calorie requirements, the most important being its bodyweight, activeness, individual nature and age. In the case of a breeding bitch, gestation and lactation make specially high demands. A young puppy may need over 100 calories a day for every pound it weighs. An inactive old dog of a large breed metabolizes at less than a quarter of this rate, although *total* calorie requirement is much higher, owing to the greater bodyweight. An adult pet dog weighing 20–25 lb (about 10 kg) usually needs 600–750 calories a day whereas a Labrador or Alsatian may need up to 2,000 calories. The following table gives the average calories needed for adult dogs of various weights taking light exercise as pets.

Body Weight lb	Representative Breed	Average No. of Calories needed per day
5	Pomeranian	250
10	Miniature Dachshund	430
20	Fox Terrier	700
35	Staffordshire Bull Terrier	1,000
50	Bulldog	1,250
65	Retriever	1,500
80	Alsatian	1,750
100	Bloodhound	2,100
140	Great Dane	2,800

Dry dog foods (both biscuit and meals) supply about 1,600 calories per pound of food. The calorie value of meats and meat offals varies considerably according to water and fat content. Most tinned dog meats provide 400–600 calories a pound.

2. Water

All living things need water. About two-thirds of a dog, by weight, is water and no vital process can take place in its absence. Through respiration, perspiration, excretion and secretion water is continually being lost and must be replaced. The water requirement varies enormously with a dog's size, activity and condition. For a medium-sized dog it is likely to exceed a quart (1,130 ml) a day. Some of this water is present in the food eaten and some is produced by digestion of food but the remainder (usually the majority) must be given as drinking water.

3. Protein

Protein is the basic building material of which the animal body is constructed. Water acts as a solvent and vehicle for transport, but protein provides the structure for such diverse tissues as muscle, hair, blood and the internal organs. Even the skeleton, although owing its rigidity to mineral matter, is developed by the activity of living protein-rich cells.

Like all other animals, the dog is unable to make protein from non-protein foodstuffs and therefore must receive a sufficient quantity of protein in its diet. The quality of the protein is also important. It must be digestible but it must also have a suitable composition in terms of 'amino-acids': these are the simple chemical substances from which all proteins are built up. Some of these amino-acids (there are about twenty altogether) can be made in the animal body from other amino-acids, but some – the 'essential' amino-acids – cannot, and must be provided by the protein of the diet. In general, proteins from animal sources (eggs, milk, meat and fish) are richer in essential amino-acids than vegetable proteins, and are said to be of higher quality or 'biological value'.

The adult dog needs about 20% of protein in its diet, expressed as a proportion of the weight of dry matter in the food. About half of this protein should be from animal sources. Alternatively it can be said that the dog needs $1\frac{1}{2}$–2 grams of dietary protein per pound bodyweight per day.

4. Fat

Fat is a valuable source of energy (calories). By increasing the fat content of a diet it is possible to reduce the bulk of food required. This is important in compounding very high energy diets, as required by sledge dogs. For most dogs, however, a dietary fat content of 5–10% (based on the food's dry matter) is sufficient.

Fat has other functions than the supply of calories. Some constituents of fats have a vital role in maintaining healthy skin and coat condition. These constituents, referred to as 'essential fatty acids' or 'polyunsaturates' are more concentrated in some fats than others, cod liver oil and such vegetable oils as wheatgerm and cottonseed oils being a particularly rich source.

Finally, fat is highly palatable to dogs, and provides a means of making diets more acceptable.

5. Carbohydrate

Carbohydrate is the technical term for starch and sugars. It also includes cellulose, which is not digestible by the dog. Carbohydrate is the cheapest source of energy in food. Although carbohydrate is not essential in itself to a dog, diets free from it are expensive and may led to nutritional diseases through a surplus of the other essential nutrients, protein, fat and minerals. In practice, when all other nutritional requirements have been satisfied, the remainder of the diet (about 70% of the dry matter) may consist of digestible carbohydrate. There is no truth in the idea that the dog cannot digest starch. Even raw starch is partly assimilated and cooked starch undergoes complete digestion as in man. It follows that both bread and cooked potato can form part of a balanced canine diet.

The fibrous parts of plant foods (e.g. wheat bran and vegetable leaves) consist mainly of cellulose which is not digested. Nevertheless a small proportion of fibre in the diet is useful in providing bulk for the stools.

6. Vitamins

The dog requires two groups of vitamins:

(i) the 'fat-soluble' vitamins A, D and E;
(ii) the 'water-soluble' vitamins of the B group (about ten in number).

A normal healthy dog does not need vitamin C (ascorbic acid) being able to make its own in the body. Indeed, only man, some monkeys and the lowly guinea pig among all the mammals are known to need ascorbic acid. Vitamin K also is probably not needed as a dietary constituent.

A properly balanced diet of natural foodstuffs will usually contain adequate amounts of vitamins for the adult dog. Liver is a rich source of all vitamins. Milk supplies lesser amounts but is a useful source of vitamins A and B_2 (riboflavin). The B group occurs in meat and yeast. Cereals supply vitamin B_1 (thiamin).

The fish liver oils contain remarkably high levels of vitamins A and D and must be given with discretion. Surpluses of vitamin A are stored in the body and in excess can cause disease. Excess vitamin D, instead of assisting formation of bone, actually causes bone matter to disperse.

7. Minerals

Like vitamins, minerals are required in relatively small amounts. They differ in being immutable chemical elements instead of biological substances. About a dozen mineral elements are known to be needed by the dog.

Calcium, in the form of calcium phosphate, is the major constituent of bones and teeth. Phosphorus, as phosphate, also has important functions in the basic processes of digestion and growth. Sodium and chlorine are combined as common salt, which helps to regulate the movement of water within the body. Magnesium and potassium salts occur inside the tissue cells and are also concerned with water transfer. Magnesium is a minor constituent of bone. Iron is a constituent of the red pigment of blood and hence of enzymes concerned with respiration. Copper, manganese and zinc are also enzyme constituents. Cobalt occurs in vitamin B_{12}, the anti-pernicious anaemia vitamin. Fluorine occurs in the teeth, in minute amounts, and helps to protect them from decay. Sulphur is a constituent of the essential amino-acid methionine and of some other body substances.

In general, minerals are poorly absorbed from food, but a sensible diet will supply adequate amounts of all except calcium, phosphorus and possibly salt. The only natural source of calcium is bone, either fresh or processed as steamed bone flour. The total dry matter of a balanced diet should contain about 2% calcium phosphate and 1% common salt by weight.

8. Composition of traditional dog foods

The following chart summarizes the nutritive value of some of the natural foodstuffs most commonly fed to dogs. Each is analysed as a source of the five main groups of nutrients: energy, protein, fat, vitamins and minerals.

Nutritive value of foods for dogs:

Food	Energy	Protein	Fat	Vitamins	Minerals
Meat	2	3	2	1	–
Liver	2	3	1	3	–
Milk	1	1	1	1	1
Bones	1	1	1	–	3
Cereals	3	1	–	1	–

1 indicates an adequate but not rich source of the nutrient(s);
2 indicates a valuable source of the nutrient(s);
3 indicates a rich source of the nutrient(s).

A balanced diet is built up by choosing foods which together cover all needs. For example, a diet of meat, cereals and bones, plus a little liver to safeguard the vitamin level and drinking water freely available, is complete and balanced. This leads to the detailed consideration of practical feeding which follows.

Since the domestic dog is omnivorous, many diets can be devised to meet its nutritional requirements. In practice, however, the diet need not be varied widely as dogs are creatures of habit, usually content to eat the same food day after day. The sensible method for feeding an adult dog is to find a diet which is liked, and on which the animal thrives, and to vary this as little as possible. Most dogs do well on a diet of water, meat, biscuit and an occasional bone, with one main meal a day and no snacks.

Because of the bewildering variety of dog foods available, and the conflicting advice sometimes given, a simple review of practical canine dietetics is necessary.

The Menu

Water must be supplied fresh each day. A heavy earthenware bowl is the most satisfactory container. It should be replenished as necessary throughout the day and washed out thoroughly once a day.

Meat of almost any kind is an excellent source of protein and highly palatable to dogs. It should always be cooked. A dog can digest raw meat and offals, and may even prefer carrion or putrefying meat, but there is the danger, particularly in hot weather, of food poisoning or contamination with parasites and their eggs. Meat offals such as tripe (paunch), lung (lights), spleen (melts), heart and kidney all provide good protein. Liver, in addition, is rich in vitamins but should not constitute more than 5% of the total diet owing to its laxative properties and the possibility of addiction. Offals from cattle, sheep and pig are all suitable, again after cooking to destroy bacteria and parasites. Meat alone does not provide an adequate diet, being deficient in several nutrients and also liable to put an excessive strain on the kidneys.

Milk, fish and eggs are other valuable protein foods which may be used to tempt a fussy feeder. Both fish and eggs should be cooked. Milk in excess is laxative. Tinned meat for dogs is readily available.

Some brands are supplemented with cereal, vitamins and minerals so as to make a complete food, but the majority are designed for mixing with cereal foods. Tins have the advantages of convenience (the contents are pre-cooked, sterile and keep indefinitely) and hygiene. A recent survey showed that over 60% of owners in the U.K. give their dogs tinned meat every day.

Another form of meat in the pet shops is the frozen block of minced cooked offal. Such food is as nutritious as fresh meat, but more hazardous from the hygiene aspect than tinned meat. Other manufacturers preserve minced meat with such chemicals as sulphite and benzoic acid. These products may prove unpalatable to an individual dog and have a limited shelf-life unless sealed in heat-resistant film and cooked.

Biscuits and Meals

It is customary to include a proportion of cereal-based foods in a dog's diet. They help to meet calorie needs at a relatively low cost and also contain fibre which adds bulk to the stools. These cereal foods are sold as biscuits, kibbled meals and loose meals. The last-named are comparatively rare; they consist of a mixture of flaked maize, wheat and other cereals with dry meat meal, dried yeast, skimmed milk powder, bone meal and possibly added fat and vitamins. The biscuits and meals are based on wheaten flour, frequently supplemented with vitamins and minerals to help to balance a meat diet. A mixture of equal parts by weight of meat with a supplemented biscuit or meal is an excellent diet for any healthy dog.

Some meals are made, not from a biscuit dough, but by extrusion of a damp mass of the ingredients under high temperature and pressure. The material expands with the escape of steam as it is extruded through holes in a die plate and is cut off as pellets of any desired size. These so-called expanded meals are usually formulated to be nutritionally complete and are popular in the U.S.A. They can be produced in a variety of shapes and are both convenient and economical since no other food is needed. Disadvantages are the lack of palatability for some dogs and a tendency to cause bulky soft stools.

The question arises with biscuits and meals whether to feed them dry or moistened in water or gravy. There is no objection to dry feeding although a dog used to wet food may need a gradual transition. Dry crunchy food may assist through abrasion in keeping the dog's teeth and gums in good condition. Wetting food, however, makes it more palatable. If dry feeding is adopted it is essential that drinking water be freely available at all times.

Bones

Gnawing a bone gives most dogs enjoyment. Some nourishment is provided and gnawing helps to keep the teeth clean and shiny. The bone should be as large as the dog can just carry and should first be boiled for a few minutes. A sawn-up marrow bone is ideal. Smaller bones may splinter and stick in a dog's throat or cause internal injury. Fish, rabbit and poultry bones should never be given. Where more than one dog is kept bones can cause serious fighting. Even docile pet dogs should be given their bones in separate rooms.

Fruit and vegetables

There is no evidence that a healthy dog's diet must contain fruit or vegetables. Vitamin C is not needed. Nevertheless nearly all dogs eat grass at times, as an emetic or purgative, and a proportion of green vegetables in the diet may be of value for the laxative effect. Owing to the low calorie value and high roughage content this proportion should be small. Starchy vegetables, notably the potato, if cooked are an alternative source of energy food to cereals and may be fed mixed with meat or other protein foods. Cooked potato has only about one quarter the energy value of dry biscuits and meals.

Other foods

'Soft-moist' products are popular in the U.S.A. and appear from time to time in the U.K. They consist of meat preserved with sugar and similar substances, much as fruit is preserved with sugar to make jam. Vitamins and minerals may be added. Soft-moist foods can be made to simulate meat or bacon as mince, slices, dice or chunks. They are convenient and reasonably palatable but contain several chemical preservatives in addition to sugar. Bread was mentioned earlier. It contains 35–40% water and is a source of energy, some protein and fat, the B vitamins (especially thiamin), calcium and iron. Three parts fresh bread by weight replace two parts dry biscuit.

Table scraps have the disadvantages of great variability and generally low nutritive value – pieces of gristle, stalks of vegetables, etc. They should never form more than a small proportion of the total diet.

Tea, coffee and beer are sometimes given to and accepted by dogs who may even acquire their owners' taste for these drinks. There is no harm if moderation is exercised; advice which applies equally to the owners!

Foods to avoid

There are few foods for humans which a dog will not accept and digest. It is important to avoid an excess of some foods lest the diet become unbalanced. Items which should be given in moderation if at all are:

1. Raw white of egg and raw whole herring which contain anti-vitamin factors.
2. Splintery bones.
3. Raw meats and offals, especially in hot weather.
4. Chocolates, sweets, sweet biscuits and sweet puddings which are bad for the teeth. In excess they will unbalance the diet and possibly induce a tendency to diabetes. An occasional chocolate drop may be useful as a reward for training purposes but savoury snacks are equally effective.

The dog has a large stomach for its size and is able to ingest big meals at relatively infrequent intervals. Healthy adult dogs of normal size and above need only one meal a day. A toy dog needs relatively more food and may be given two meals a day. There is no harm in giving any dog more than one meal a day, provided that the quantities are adjusted to avoid overfeeding. A convenient system is a main meal of meat with cereal and a second lighter meal of biscuits, perhaps with milk. Some owners starve their dogs for one day a week. The idea may be that an animal is unlikely to overeat sufficiently on the other six days to make up the deficit and lay down a surplus as fatty tissue. No harm will come to a healthy dog, but regulation of daily intake according to bodyweight is a more scientific method of controlling diet.

Meals may be given at any time convenient to household or kennel routine. It is important to keep to the established system. All dogs expect their meals at the usual hour. Working dogs are usually fed in the evening, but morning feeds reduce the risk of night-time accidents!

Snacks between meals should be avoided, except training titbits, or overfeeding results. It is a matter of the owner's convenience where meals are given. The kitchen floor is an obvious place: since the average dog takes only minutes to finish its food the problem of finding space hardly arises. Unfinished food should not be left down. It can be saved for a second meal the same day, if this is the regime, but otherwise should be discarded. Depending on the dog's size, almost any container of reasonable weight will serve as a feeding dish, but an energetic dog will push a small plastic bowl all over the floor. For large dogs, or more than one dog, baking tins are admirable. If dogs are fed together, ensure each gets his share. Water in a heavy earthenware bowl with a permanent, accessible site should always be available. The amount of food needed is determined mainly by the dog's natural weight, that is, the weight at which it is in peak physical condition for an active, but not excessively strenuous life. Other factors are the age, state of health, activeness and individual nature of the animal, and the ambient temperature. (The extra requirements for breeding are described in Chapter 12.) The difficulty of prescribing precise quantities is the composition of the food, in particular its water content. For example, one pound of a complete, balanced dry food is equal to at least two pounds of a wet food such as meat. The feeding chart shows the average amount of food needed each day by dogs of various sizes receiving light exercise as pets. The cost of feeding is an important consideration for any dog owner. It should be stressed that a nutritionally complete diet is not necessarily expensive. Of the diets shown in the Chart, No. 1 is the cheapest and No. 3 the most expensive, but all three are balanced. Cost tends to be related to palatability. Not surprisingly, most dogs find meat and other animal products highly palatable. If allowed to become addicted to such foods, they will be much more expensive to feed than is necessary to maintain perfect health and condition.

Feeding Chart for Adult House Dogs
Average Quantity of Food needed each Day

Representative Breeds	*Approx. Weight of Dog*	DIET 1 *Complete Dry Meal*	DIET 2 *Equal parts Meat and Biscuit* TOTAL	DIET 3 *Complete Canned Food*
	lb	*lb oz*	*lb oz*	*lb oz*
Chihuahua	2	0 1½	0 2½	0 6
Pomeranian, Maltese	5	0 2½	0 4	0 10
Yorkshire Terrier, Toy Poodle	8	0 3½	0 6	0 14
Pekingese, Papillon, Miniature Dachshund	10	0 4	0 7	1 0
Cairn Terrier, Miniature Poodle, Shetland Sheepdog	15	0 5½	0 9	1 6
Corgi, Dachshund, Fox Terrier, Scottie, Whippet, West Highland Terrier	20	0 7	0 11	1 12

Cocker Spaniel, Irish Terrier	25	0	8	0	13	2 0
Beagle, Kerry Blue, Schnauzer	30	0	9	0	14	2 4
Bull Terrier, Springer Spaniel	40	0	11	1	2	2 12
Airedale, Bulldog, Chow Chow, Dalmatian	50	0	13	1	5	3 4
Boxer, Greyhound, Retrievers, Setters	60	0	15	1	8	3 12
Alsatian	70	1	1	1	11	4 4
Rhodesian Ridgeback	80	1	3	1	14	4 12
Bloodhound, Bullmastiff, Pyrenean Mountain Dog	100	1	7	2	4	5 12
Great Dane, Mastiff, Newfoundland	150	2	0	3	2	8 0
St. Bernard	190	2	8	4	0	10 0

NOTE: The standard tin of dog food contains about 15 oz, the so-called 'handy' size contains about 7 oz.

8 | Exercise

As will have been seen in the last chapter, the connection between exercise and feeding is close. At its simplest, a dog which takes an enormous amount of exercise, and by this is meant those who pull sledges over arctic wastes, pursue foxes and hunt for eight hours or patrol all night in the jungle, burn up a lot of energy. They therefore need a lot more food than the average pet.

But this should not be taken to mean that a fat and over-fed dog can be reduced to healthy normalcy by even the most vigorous exercise most pet owners would normally give it. The only practical way to reduce weight, and obviously this also applies to humans, is to reduce food intake.

Look upon exercise as a recreation, a means of getting fresh air into the lungs, a way of maintaining an interest in life, in stimulating both mentally and physically, in toning muscles and mind. Without exercise and by that is meant regular and adequate exercise, dogs invariably become soft, fat and mentally dull.

Puppies

Oddly enough the only time in their lives that dogs do not want organized exercise is the time when most of them get it! In many cases as soon as a new owner has bought a puppy he also buys a collar and lead and attempts to take it for walks. Perhaps not unnaturally, these youngsters, unwilling and in many cases frightened, refuse to co-operate. They sit on the pavement and dig their toes in. Some few are then dragged along for their pains.

The truth is that puppies exercise themselves in their own way and at their own time. The usual pattern is that after a sleep they wake up, play, run around, dig, burrow, jump and generally get

into mischief. When they are very young – that is four or five weeks – this period of activity only lasts for half an hour or so. It is promptly followed by a sleep!

During what might be called their teenage – that is from two to six months – the pattern remains much the same except that their periods of wakefulness are longer, say a couple of hours at a time, but they carry on with the same habit of dropping into a sleep with very little warning.

From this it follows that the last thing they want or should be subjected to, is long, steady walks on a lead. It is extremely tiring for them, frequently boring as they have yet to develop an understanding of and an interest in the outside world, and possibly harmful to their bone formation in that, being unnatural, it imposes stresses and strains that they would have the instinct to avoid if left to their own devices.

From six months old

From six months onwards, however, perhaps nine or even twelve months in the case of the massive and therefore slow maturing breeds, they begin to like the idea of formal exercise and look forward to it. The ideal is an hour or so twice a day at the same time so that it can be both anticipated and enjoyed. The worst is a once-weekly run of several hours because their muscles are unaccustomed to such bursts and they, like ourselves, feel stiff after it.

In general then, a visit to the shops in the morning and a walk round a few blocks to post a letter in the evening is immeasurably better than eight hours on a moor on Sunday.

Oddly enough, as with feeding, dogs do not seem to require variety. They are more than content to go for the same walk every night. Indeed they appear to enjoy more actively those places they know best.

Control

Some of their exercise should be on a lead because this has the effect of muscling them up generally. Some of it, however, should be free, although this is not to say uncontrolled. All dogs like galloping, chasing birds which they have no hope of catching, digging for imaginary rabbits and generally letting off steam. All this is most desirable. What is undesirable, however, is that they should be allowed to make a nuisance of themselves by either harassing human beings, other dogs or, worst of all, livestock. The question of livestock deserves special emphasis. The farm community is in constant protest about the very substantial amount of damage done each year to cattle and sheep in particular by pet dogs. These dogs, although not killers at heart, do all too often succeed in killing. If, for example, they chase cows which are in calf the probability is that they will lose their calves. If they chase sheep, then regrettably once again the sheep not merely lose their young but often lose their own lives because they die remarkably quickly when they are subjected to non-stop running.

Chasing farm livestock is of course great fun for a dog. They quickly sense there is no danger in it but a good deal of satisfaction. If the stock did not run the game would soon come to an end; but they do run. And if they are chickens they additionally make the most delicious and stimulating clucking noises. So the dogs keep chasing them.

Inevitably it is generally town dogs who do most of the damage on their rare expeditions to the countryside and this because most country dogs have perforce been cured of this dangerous habit in their youth. It is worth mentioning in passing that the alternative to cure can be death because a farmer is not only entitled by law to shoot to protect his stock, but frequently does so. Who can blame him?

Unrestricted freedom, that is uncontrolled exercise in towns is just as dangerous but in a different way. The danger here is to traffic and the figures produced by the police show that an alarming number of accidents on the road are caused by dogs. This problem has become so acute in certain towns that a complete ban has been placed on dogs being exercised on the roads unless on a lead. If dog owners do not want the liberty of dogs to be

further restricted by an extension of the districts covered by this order then they must take particular pains to ensure that their own dog never offends.

Whether in town or countryside no dog should ever be allowed out alone. At best it is a passing danger; at worst it may be on the way to becoming a permanent stray, because not all 'strays' are born as such. As Shakespeare might have said: 'Some dogs are born to straying; others have it thrust upon them.' The born ones can never really settle. They seem to have more than a touch of gypsy in their soul. They are always restless indoors; they have an inborn urge to move on.

Statistics from dogs' homes indicate that some 97% of strays handed in are mongrels or crossbreds. Only 3% are pedigree pooches. Maybe it's not too difficult to guess why this should be. Inevitably, most mongrels are bred on the streets. Arranged and planned matings must be the exception. Their fathers were Casanovas, and successful ones, before them. These dads who wrote their own charters had a lifetime of roaming, traffic dodging, scavenging, fighting, loving, etc., behind them. Is it surprising that their offspring frequently inherit those same anti-social inclinations?

The statistics, however, do not mean that no blue-blooded dog ever develops wanderlust or gets lost. They do. But being potentially valuable, they frequently finish up in front of somebody else's fire instead of in the dog pound.

So dogs must never be allowed out unsupervised. Not even in the garden. Most dogs could teach Houdini tricks!

While this problem, by the nature of things, is more marked in the male dog, it is in many ways more troublesome in the female. True, bitches are not normally in the habit of wandering far from home but if they are allowed out alone during their breeding season there is no doubt that they will conceive and bear mongrel puppies. Without debating here whether or not mongrel puppies are desirable it is generally admitted by true dog lovers that their indiscriminate production is undesirable, because all too few of them are fortunate enough to find good homes. It is a sad fact but true that we usually value more those things which cost us money, and treat with less respect those which we acquired without the painful necessity of paying for them.

While the subject of nuisance to neighbours is not directly connected with exercise, here may be as good a time as any to deal with it because dogs which have less opportunity to let off steam during walks are more liable to cause a nuisance by barking in the house or garden than others.

Barking at neighbours through the garden fence is a pernicious habit and should be checked; checked in the most firm manner possible with the dog being in no doubt at all that such behaviour will not be tolerated. Dogs who bark indoors usually do this in the absence of their owner. They do it because they have never been trained to stay alone in the house.

9 | Health

First let it be said that nothing in this chapter is intended to persuade you to attempt either to diagnose or treat dogs' ailments. The whole purpose of it is to help you to recognize the principal ailments, to understand their seriousness and to help you assist your veterinary surgeon in his efforts to cure them.

Home treatments and home cures, even with the advice of that well-meaning 'doggy' friend, are rarely successful. They can even be disastrous because they result in delay. And in the case of illness the one thing you do not have is time. What starts as a relatively simple illness can become a serious one if not treated quickly.

The pet owner must realize that the veterinary surgeon is a dog's best friend. He can also be a dog owner's best friend. There are 5,000 veterinarians practising in Great Britain today and their high degree of professional skill ensures that our dogs can be the best cared for in Europe. None of them, however, is capable of performing miracles. They must be given a fair chance to start healing the sick while there is still hope.

But before we get down to specific ailments, a few general principles on the maintenance of a healthy dog are given below. Follow these and you have a good chance of never owning a sick one!

1. Feed good food regularly and at the same time each day. (See 'Feeding' for enlargement.)
2. Keep food and feeding utensils scrupulously clean.
3. Never give small, i.e. chop, game or poultry bones.
4. Ensure an adequate supply of fresh air and exercise.
5. Groom regularly and preferably daily.
6. Have fresh, clean water available at all times.

Given attention to the above simple rules, it is likely that the biggest risk to your dog is one of those accidents which are said to happen in even the best regulated families. These can, and all too frequently do, occur without warning. In a crisis it is important to establish a system of priorities. And clearly the first requirement is to summon skilled aid. Next it is important to keep the patient alive and well until that aid can reach you.

It is worth repeating. If disaster strikes, telephone or ask somebody else to telephone your veterinary surgeon. Unless he gives precise instructions to the contrary, be governed from then until his arrival by the following general principles:

Whenever possible remove the cause of the injury.
Attend to haemorrhages at once.
Free air passages from obstruction.
Keep the patient warm.

Allow the animal to assume the most comfortable position by itself, supporting any injured part with a coat or blanket to avoid further damage.

If possible cover wounds with a clean dressing; a clean handkerchief will do in an emergency.

If an animal must be moved, handle so as to ensure that no further injury is caused. Injured limbs are best kept uppermost. And remember, although the animal may normally be docile, he can react differently when hurt and in pain. Restraint may be necessary and taping or tying a dog's mouth is the simplest way to avoid being bitten.

Medicines frequently require both skill and patience to administer. Obviously they should not be wasted nor should they be given in such a way as to harm the patient. Solid medicines such as pills or tablets are usually administered by placing them gently at the back of the dog's tongue, holding the jaws together until swallowed. Massaging the throat usually ensures rapid swallowing. Alternatively, enclose the pill in a piece of meat which most dogs bolt immediately. To allay suspicion give some untreated meat first.

When administering liquid medicines, some care must be taken to avoid the fluid going down the wrong way and into the lungs. Hold the head high (but not too high) leaving the tongue com-

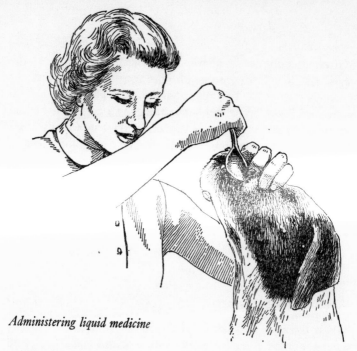

Administering liquid medicine

pletely free. Should the dog attempt to cough, release the head immediately. When giving liquid, proceed slowly, distending the cheek with one finger in order to make a pouch into which the fluid can be poured bit by bit. It is unnecessary to open his mouth; the fluid will readily find its way between his teeth.

Although powders are an easy and safe way of giving medicines, the contents must not be disagreeable in taste or smell, otherwise they will be refused. They can be given in cold food or drinking water or mixed with sugar. They may also be placed on the tongue; but beware of the possible blow-back!

Nursing is of the greatest importance in the successful treatment of a sick dog. If done at home, ensure that the patient has a comfortable bed away from draughts. Only stone hot water bottles should be used and since burns happen easily, see that they are not too hot. They should be covered with a blanket, or enclosed in an old sock. 'Pig lamps' or infra-red lamps are the safest should extra heat be required. These should be high enough so that the dog does not touch them when standing up. Endeavour to keep the room at a constant temperature and change soiled bedding. Never force food or liquids down a dog as coaxing and encouragement are usually sufficient. Water however, should always be available, unless ordered otherwise. If the dog is very ill, small amounts may be gently spooned into his mouth.

Quietness and subdued light are advisable. If the dog is unable to stand he may be carried to and supported over newspapers, or, if the weather is reasonable, into the garden, to relieve himself.

Recumbent dogs should be turned over on to the other side at least twelve times daily to prevent bed sores. The eyes, nose and orifices should be cleaned at least once a day and more often if necessary. In other words, nurse your dog as you would a child. It gives a pet the will to live.

Geriatrics means simply the changes brought about by old age. Like humans, animals are subject to degenerative alterations due to old age. And as with humans, these vary greatly. One dog may be old at six or seven, whilst another is sprightly and full of life at twelve. Generally speaking, the smaller breeds often live longer than the larger. Normally dogs start ageing when they are about eight, and although a dog's average life span is considered to be around ten years, many live much longer, even up to the age of twenty.

The usual manifestations of old age are a slowing up process. The dog no longer does all the things he once did. He will tire more easily on long walks, become disinclined to rush about, might become a little deaf and maybe suffer from impaired sight. This is accompanied by a greying muzzle and frequently discoloured, tartar-encrusted and loose teeth.

Apart from these outward signs, various changes take place inside the body. The heart may not be as strong, and valvular trouble is not uncommon. The dog's digestion might not be so active and his joints may become stiff. His kidneys might not function as efficiently. As with us humans, so with our dogs! And since we cannot stop this ageing process, we must do what we can to mitigate its discomforts.

If avoidable, old dogs should not be sent to kennels. With age they become even more attached to owners and surroundings than do their younger brethren. Regardless of kennel owners' kindness, nothing compensates for the loss of companionship which you alone can give the dog.

If, on veterinary advice, your dog's feeding habits or mode of

Applying artificial respiration

life must be changed, do it gradually. Reduce his walks slowly
and if the problem is diet, change this by degrees. Instead of
three biscuits, cut them to two and finally one.

Lastly, should old age produce some complaint that is painful
or too difficult for him to be happy with, don't hesitate to have
him put out of his misery. The end can be painless. For the
patient that is. Never for the owner.

A few common ailments and details of the usual treatment
follow in alphabetical order.

ARTIFICIAL RESPIRATION: First open the mouth, then, holding the tongue gently pull it forwards, and then let it fall back.
Repeat slowly several times. In the case of drowning, dispose of
water and assist lung expansion by holding the dog by its hind
legs and swinging it back and forth. Mouth to mouth breathing
may also be tried. Alternatively lay the animal on its side, then
with the hands widely spread push on the chest and release at
regular intervals. Do this fairly slowly, say counting up to three
after the pressure, then release. Artificial respiration is a very
slow process so do not give up too quickly.

ASPHYXIA: There are many causes for this, such as an obstruction of the air passage by a foreign body or it may be caused by the tongue folding backwards etc. Asphyxia may be partial or complete and treatment consists of removing the cause when possible, the application of artificial respiration and the inhalation of oxygen.

BURNS AND SCALDS: These are always painful and if extensive often result in shock. Veterinary attention is essential, but meanwhile only apply a clean dressing and keep the dog quiet and warm.

CANINE VIRUS HEPATITIS is a virus disease. Symptoms vary but a sudden dullness and a very high temperature, intense thirst, enlarged tonsils, abdominal tenderness, vomiting, are all possible pointers. The infection is spread mainly by urine. Sometimes the disease appears in a subacute form, an example of which is sometimes called 'blue eye', i.e. a dense opacity. Admittedly these opacities can be caused by other conditions than canine virus hepatitis infection but play safe by seeking assistance. Dogs can be vaccinated against this disease.

CHOKING is often associated with a bone becoming lodged at the back of the throat. Try to remove this but remember the risk of being bitten.

DISTEMPER: Canine distemper, caused by a virus, is alas, the most common canine disease. It usually affects young animals but older ones are also at risk. The property of this virus is that it invades and multiplies in the tissues of the nervous system, the incubation period being from ten to twenty days.

The initial symptom is a rise in body temperature, which may only last about twenty-four hours. During this period the dog may miss a meal or two, a phase often overlooked by owners. When the temperature returns to normal the animal again appears healthy. However, ten days later signs of the disease reappear. These symptoms vary from one outbreak to the next. The following symptoms demand immediate and skilled examination: sneezing, coughing, loss of appetite, diarrhoea, vomiting and discharge from the nose and eyes – plus a loss of bounce and alertness. The distemper symptoms may last for several weeks, and a distressing factor is that nervous symptoms may develop weeks after apparent recovery.

The risk of death from distemper is very high and prevention is better than cure. All dogs should be vaccinated against distemper and the other virus diseases such as canine virus hepatitis, at twelve weeks.

DROWNING: The treatment is to remove foreign matter from around the nose and mouth. If possible, hold up the dog by his hind legs for a few seconds to allow water to drain from his nostrils; then apply artificial respiration. On recovery, keep him warm and dry, giving warm drinks at regular intervals.

EAR: An organ vulnerable to injuries which can lead to complications if neglected.

ECZEMA: Eczema is perhaps best described by saying that it is an inflammation of the skin, non-contagious, and often limited to one particular area of the body. It is characterized at first by very small vesicles which contain fluid. This condition is accompanied by an irritation which causes scratching so setting up further irritation and possibly secondary infection.

In some cases it may be due to internal causes, such as indigestion or gastric upset. Again, the condition may be caused by nerves. Other possible causes are chemical irritants, external irritants such as dirt, matted hair close to the skin and bathing with irritating soap. These different causes bring different manifestations so that the eczema may be active, or chronic – wet or dry.

Eczema should never be neglected. And usually it can be cured.

ELECTRIC SHOCK is usually caused by animals biting through live wires. Don't touch your dog until you have turned off the current and pulled out the plug. Since electrocuted animals often urinate, avoid stepping into pools, since water is a conductor of electricity. Apply artificial respiration immediately.

EYE: A delicate organ easily damaged by blows, grass seeds, scalds, etc. Even a minor injury may lead to blindness if not attended to promptly by a veterinary surgeon.

FITS may be caused by many different agents. Whilst a fit is in progress the animal should be confined where it is unlikely to damage itself. Restraint may be necessary but take care not to get bitten. Professional help is essential.

FOREIGN BODIES: Pieces of stick, bones and needles frequently lodge in dogs' mouths. They may be suspected if the dog rubs the sides of his mouth frantically with his paws. Profuse salivation may occur. Immediate attempts should be made to remove the foreign body. Sometimes foreign bodies lodge in the pharynx or the gullet which requires prompt veterinary attention. Foreign bodies such as blades of grass or splinters of wood can lodge between the teeth. If you can see them they should be removed.

FRACTURES vary in severity and form, but in all cases the primary treatment consists in the prevention of further injury to the broken bone and its surrounding tissues – and easing the pain. Whenever a fracture is suspected make the dog as comfortable as possible, restrict movement and ensure warmth. Do not make any attempt to set the broken bone.

HAEMORRHAGE: is caused usually by an injury, and consists of bleeding from any part of the body. It may also occur in some illnesses. It must be regarded as serious because even slight haemorrhages continued over a long period can result in death. The bleeding may be from an artery or vein, and the general symptoms vary according to the amount of blood lost and the rate at which this has happened. The immediate result of haemorrhage is shock, recognized by a pallor of the gums, the insides of the lips, and the insides of the lower eyelids. The patient will be dull and listless, the pulse rapid and feeble, and the skin and legs cool. Breathing may become rapid, there may be a staggering gait, or complete collapse, caused by a sub-normal temperature.

First aid treatment for excessive bleeding consists of either direct or indirect pressure:

(a) Direct (digital) pressure, e.g. press as hard as possible with your fingers on the wound.

(b) Indirect pressure by means of a pad or bandage.

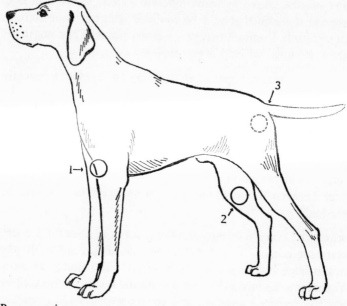

Pressure points

The 'pressure points' are in those parts of the body where it is possible to apply pressure on to an artery which is near to a bone.
    In dogs these points are:

1. The site of the brachial artery, about 1 to 1½ inches above the elbow joint. Pressure here will control bleeding from below the elbow.
2. The femoral artery, just below the stifle joint (equivalent to the human knee joint) on the inside of the thigh.
3. The coccygeal artery is at the root of the tail on the underside.

    Tourniquets should be applied only in cases of severe bleeding which cannot be controlled by any other method. Usually, a tourniquet is a flat rubber bandage, but in emergency one can be improvised by twisting a scarf or handkerchief around firmly just above the wound, and winding it with a stick or pencil. The pressure should be only sufficient to control the haemorrhage, and the tourniquet must not be left on for more than 15 minutes. After this release it, and re-apply if the bleeding continues.

HEART ATTACKS: Collapse associated with heart disease usually is the result of excitement possibly following exercise. In most cases, the loss of consciousness is sudden. However, mild cases may be preceded by a bout of coughing, after which the dog will stand still, swaying slightly. Recovery in such cases takes place quickly, and when consciousness returns an alcoholic stimulant may be given. A veterinary check is essential.

HEAT AND SUNSTROKE: These are very common conditions in dogs – particularly those with short muzzles such as bulldogs. The signs are vomiting, profuse salivation, weakness of the limbs, a staggering gait and finally collapse. Put the patient in a cool place and apply anything cold. Ice or cold water can be applied to the head, neck and shoulders, or cold water poured over the dog. On recovery, the dog should be dried, placed in a cool room and encouraged to drink.

LEPTOSPIROSIS: This is an acute infection of which there are two types: leptospirosis ictohaemorrhagica and leptospirosis canicola.

The first is often called 'yellows' by huntsmen and kennelmen because one of the symptoms is jaundice. The disease is highly infectious. During the active stage, and following recovery, many dogs act as carriers via their urine. Rats also serve as reservoirs of the infection and spread it either by direct contact or by contamination of food and water via their urine and faeces.

The incubation period is from five to fifteen days and the disease begins suddenly. It is characterized by a slight weakness, refusal to eat, vomiting and a temperature of 103° F to 105° F. Often there is congestion of the eyes. At this stage a differential diagnosis is sometimes difficult. The next symptom is a sudden drop in temperature when depression is more noticeable, laboured breathing and abnormal thirst. Muscular stiffness and soreness of the hind legs are frequently evident, the dog being reluctant to rise from a sitting position. If the limbs are touched he will show signs of pain. The mucous membranes of the mouth often show irregular haemorrhagic patches that look like burns and there may be difficulty in swallowing due to pharyngitis.

Later there will be deeper depression, muscular tremors and a drop to sub-normal temperature coupled with abdominal pain and liquid blood-stained stools. Urination will be frequent; the eyes sunken and the pulse small and thready. In fatal cases death usually takes place in from five to ten days after the onset of symptoms.

Early treatment with an adequate use of antibiotics reduces the mortality risk considerably. Good care and nursing are essential, and a soft, light diet consisting mainly of milk and broth should be given little and often. Vaccination is available.

This disease can be passed on to man via the urine and faeces of sick dogs so if your hands become contaminated, wash them thoroughly.

LOSS OF CONSCIOUSNESS: The animal should be laid on its side, with the head extended and the tongue drawn out. Tight collars or coats should be removed and warmth applied plus fresh air. No attempt must be made to give fluids by the mouth and stay with your dog until professional help arrives.

MANGE: The three forms of mange which attack dogs are sarcoptic, otodectic and follicular. Sarcoptic mange is perhaps the most common of all skin diseases. It can affect all breeds at any age, and has been found in four-week-old puppies. It is highly contagious and transmitted chiefly by direct contact although it can be caught through indirect means such as from infected bedding, kennels, attendants' clothing, dirty brushes, etc. Humans can, and sometimes do, contract mange so care is necessary when handling infected dogs or material.

The primary symptom is extreme irritation of the skin. This is followed by persistent scratching and a tendency to rub along the ground and against objects. Some of these symptoms are portrayed with eczema but they are unlikely to be so intense or frequent. In mange the irritation intensifies in a warm atmosphere or when the dog is hot following exercise. Generally the first part of the body to be invaded is the head and around the eyes, on the face and outer sides of the ears. Then the condition spreads along and under the neck, chest and abdomen and so to the legs – especially elbows and hocks.

If neglected it ultimately spreads over the whole body. If mange is not treated the dog loses condition and becomes emaciated.

9   Cruft's

10 Miniature Long-haired Dachshund. Small, excellent town pet, despite hunting background

11 Pekingese puppy. Long-coated, glamorous, usually surprisingly willing to take exercise

12 Bloodhound. Outstanding tracking dog. A striking companion for those who can accommodate him

13 Beagle. Likes exercise, but given this can be happy anywhere

14a Miniature Poodle. Never moults, but coat needs regular and costly attention

14b Yorkshire Terrier. Coat needs considerable attention if to remain in perfect show condition

15a Dandie Dinmont Terrier. High-spirited, active and an enthusiastic hunter

15b Maltese. Popular toy breed whose long silky coat needs plenty of care

16a Wire-haired Fox Terrier. Good companion for children, but will not tolerate boredom

16b Smooth-haired Dachshunds. Tendency to overweight must be watched

Diagnosis, suspected from the above symptoms, may be confirmed by skin scrapings, when the parasites can be identified under a microscope. Treatment and cure in the case of sarcoptic mange is not difficult if dealt with early enough.

Otodectic mange affects only the dog's ears but like the sarcoptic variety is highly contagious and can spread rapidly. The affected animal will scratch frequently, shake his head and rub it along the ground. Usually the parasites are found deep down in the wax of the ear where they cause extreme irritation and damage the sensitive ear lining. This has been known to result in fits.

The last type of mange is follicular or demodectic mange. Whilst perhaps not so common as the other two, it is the most obstinate to treat. The parasite invades deep down into the hair follicles and sebaceous glands of the skin. It is found in all breeds but, unlike sarcoptic mange, is only mildly contagious.

Unlike the other forms of mange little skin irritation is displayed but the animal shakes himself frequently. The skin becomes bare of hair, giving off a sulphur-like odour. Sometimes the affected parts are red but they may be darkly pigmented. Treatment is difficult and lengthy and early advice should be sought.

POISONS: The diagnosis of these is difficult and expert advice should be obtained immediately. It helps if the owner is able to identify the poison to enable the correct antidote to be administered. An immediate emetic is essential, that most readily available being a strong solution of washing soda, or a piece of this forced gently down the throat. The size of the piece will vary according to the size of the dog, but it can be as large as a tenpence piece in the case of large dogs.

PULSE: This is taken by pressing the fingers (not thumb) against the artery which runs down the inside of the hind leg, the dog's normal pulse at rest being 80 to 120, the smaller the dog the higher the rate.

RING WORM: Ring worm is not uncommon in the dog. It is contagious and may be passed to man or even from man to dog.

The symptoms. It is usually first seen around the eyes, feet or

Taking a dog's pulse

sometimes the gums. The main characteristics are the formation encrusted round rings. If on the skin the hair is broken and gives the appearance of being shorter than the surrounding hair.

It can be a very serious condition and must not be neglected. Treatment is often protracted.

SNAKE BITES in Britain, usually caused by adders, resulting in a massive swelling around the injured part. The patient may show great distress and, in severe cases, collapse. Should the bite be in a limb, the application of a tourniquet may stop the poison from spreading into the blood stream.

SPRAINS are caused by tearing or stretching the ligaments and other tissues surrounding a joint. Symptoms are pain, loss of power and swelling or tenderness. Obviously the affected joint must be rested and the application of a pressure bandage reduces the swelling and immobilizes the joint.

STRAINS are the tearing or stretching of muscles, the symptoms being similar to those found in sprains and they should be treated similarly.

STROKES are caused by haemorrhage into the substance of the brain, or a clotting of blood in the brain blood vessels. Often the onset is sudden and may be accompanied by vomiting. Usually there is only partial loss of consciousness. Attempts to walk or stand are unsuccessful, the head is held to one side with the eyeballs moving to and fro. Keep the dog very quiet in a darkened room and never give stimulants.

TEMPERATURE: The dog's normal temperature is $101\frac{1}{2}°$ F but it varies slightly and in some dogs it may be 102° F. The best way to take a dog's temperature is to grease a veterinary thermometer and insert it 2 to 3 inches into the rectum. Steady the dog with one hand by holding on to his tail to avoid the risk of movement breaking the thermometer.

TRAVEL SICKNESS: This unpleasant complaint is common, usually youngsters being more susceptible than adults. There are three causes for car sickness: (1) apprehension; (2) the car's swaying motion, and (3) the window view of a moving horizon to a susceptible subject. For (2) and (3) dogs allowed to travel in the front of the car, either on the floor or the front seat, frequently effect immediate cures, but this is not advised from the road safety point of view unless the dog is very well trained. Apprehension is, of course, most often seen in nervous dogs. So first you must gain their confidence. A tried method is to coax them into the car, get in yourself and stay with them for a short time. After a few attempts, start the engine and drive the car out of the garage. Gradually increase the distances. If the foregoing fails you may have to resort to sickness antidotes and preventatives as advised by a veterinary surgeon. Either way the golden rule with a suspect case is never feed before a journey.

WASP AND BEE STINGS: The latter leave their stings in the wound, therefore these should be removed with a pair of eyebrow tweezers. Remember that bee stings are acid, and wasp stings alkaline. Therefore the antidotes for bee stings are either a solution of common washing soda or a lump of wet soda rubbed on the affected part. For wasp stings apply neat vinegar to allay the pain. Should neither soda nor vinegar be available, rub with a raw onion. (This advice applies equally to humans.)

WOUNDS: The most common of these are:

(a) An incised wound caused by a sharp cutting instrument.

(b) Lacerated wounds which are irregular in shape, have jagged edges, and sometimes loss of skin. Usually they are caused by car accidents, bites from other animals, barbed wire, gunshot wounds, or blows.

(c) Punctured wounds, caused commonly by bites, or objects such as nails, bullets, fish-hooks, thorns, etc.

Complications: The most usual dangers caused by wounds are haemorrhage, shock and septicaemia.

When dealing with wounds never apply cotton wool directly on to the affected part. A small square of gauze should always be put on before the cotton wool and the whole finally bandaged.

10 | Training

The first, and perhaps most important item on the training agenda, that is house training, has already been dealt with in Chapter 5. The author hardly thought it would wait until this stage of the book has been reached by the owner of a new puppy!

But a little more than this is necessary because the charming little savage you have brought into your house will have to share your life, and the life of your friends, for the next ten or so years. Well behaved children are popular. Badly behaved children are not. Exactly the same applies to dogs. There can be few things more irritating than spending an evening with friends whose dog behaves in a way that both offends and annoys us.

Dog owners, perhaps not unnaturally, forgive their own pets many irritating habits because they like them. They have also come to accept these irritations as normal. Other people are rarely as tolerant even if the conventions do demand a fixed smile in the face of grave provocation.

With a reasonable amount of care, however, a puppy can be brought up to behave in a civilized manner, when he will be liked and appreciated by all, particularly by his owners who will get the full pleasure which comes from owning a well behaved and therefore properly adjusted dog.

Talking of training raises in many people's minds thoughts of turning somersaults, jumping through hoops, and performing a series of stylized and somewhat boring obedience routines. Many more hold the view that a trained dog is merely a robot; an unthinking, blindly obedient machine. This is by no means true.

What is required of a family pet is that he should never make a nuisance of himself, that he should not be destructive, that he should walk to heel, sit and stay on command. This is not too much to ask and it is all very easily taught, as long as we remember that training must commence from the moment the dog enters the house.

We have already dealt with house cleanliness. Another equally elementary piece of training that requires prompt attention to avoid a prolonged battle of wills, is that of staying quietly on his own.

While most of us want our dogs with and near us they should never be allowed to take it for granted that they must be by our side for every one of our, or their, waking moments. As mentioned earlier, young puppies spend a considerable part of every day sleeping. It is better if the timing for this is to some extent regulated by the owner. Thus a youngster can reasonably be put in the kitchen, and on his own, for a couple of hours after lunch every day. There is no hardship involved because he will sleep.

The dog, having been taught right from the start (see page 144) that it is not necessarily fatal to spend an occasional hour or two alone, will soon accept it when a housewife goes shopping for an hour in the afternoon and, perhaps even more important, for two or three hours in the evening when the family goes to the cinema.

One other way of making a dog accept his owner's instructions without a battle of wills is by teaching him the simple lesson 'Go to bed'.

The average puppy loves his bed. He goes there dozens of times in a day, either to sleep, to sit down, or to play with some treasured toy. If on each occasion that he runs towards his bed you say to him 'Go to bed' he will in a very short time begin to associate the words with the act. A day or two of this and you will find that when he is running past the bed you can make him swerve into it by using this same expression: 'Go to bed'.

Two lessons have been learned. The dog has learned one, which is that your instructions are meant for him. You have learned that as long as your instructions are simple and uncomplicated they will be obeyed by the dog. You will also have learned the importance of always using the same set of words to bring about a certain course of action.

'Pop into your cot' is not good enough, neither is 'Get out of my way'. The instruction is, and it is repeated here for the fourth time to hammer home the lesson, 'Go to bed'.

We have already learned the use of the rapped out command, 'No'. It was used to stop the puppy whining when left in the kitchen. It can also be used to stop the dog doing anything of which you do not approve. For example, chewing the chair leg, tearing your clothes, chasing the family cat, threatening the postman and indeed all of the major and minor crimes which any puppy can and will, if not controlled, commit during the course of his life.

It can also be used to prevent him from developing those many other little characteristics that seem engaging in puppyhood, but quite the reverse when the dog is adult. Jumping on furniture for example. Occupying the best armchair, sleeping on your bed, jumping up to you and indeed other people, tugging at your coat when he walks. But why go on? We know what we disapprove of in dogs and the important thing is not to let them start these bad habits. 'No' is the operative word.

We now leave what might be called 'behaviour training' and go on to formal training. This usually commences at about six months of age, although this is not to say that any dog, almost regardless of age, cannot be taught to obey instructions.

An untrained dog of ten could be taught, but it would not be easy. With the older dog you would be trying to do two things at once. Trying to break the habit of many years standing which is to ignore orders. Trying at the same time to teach him what the orders meant. It can be done, but you will need more perseverance and more patience. In any case, regardless of age, the principles of teaching a dog formal obedience are the same.

So first principles with the help of the following ten basic steps. After that we get down to details:

1. Fix clearly in your mind the reasons for training. They are to ensure the dog becomes a clean, well behaved, civilized and safe companion. Untrained he is just another animal.
2. Accept that the only reward he needs is praise, a kind word and a caress. Titbits are usually unnecessary as a dog obeys to please you.

... a kind word and a caress

3. Punishment other than a rebuke is best avoided. Physical violence could lose you his respect.
4. Settle on the important things a dog should know. He should sit, lie down and stay on command, walk to heel on or off the lead, come when called and understand 'No'.
5. Choose the 'schoolroom' with care, to avoid distractions. A dog cannot concentrate when his attention is diverted.
6. Lessons must be short and sweet. Ten minutes four times a day stimulate; two hours once a week bore.
7. Always show the dog what you want done. If you are teaching the 'sit', push his hindquarters gently to the ground.
8. Repeat the command 'Sit . . . sit . . . sit', as you demonstrate to link word and action in his mind. Follow with the aforementioned 'reward'.
9. Remember that practice makes perfect. When a lesson has been absorbed, fix it by frequent practice.
10. To have value a dog must enjoy lessons. If 'school' is not interesting, your pupil will fail the eleven plus!

These bare outlines are for you. Now the bare bones will be clothed and your dog, no matter how unwilling, will be invited to take part. The system of teaching is exactly the same regardless of what lesson you decide upon. You show the dog what you want him to do, for example, put him into a sitting position if that be the lesson, repeating all the time the one simple word of command which fixes it in the dog's mind. When he has complied, no matter how unwillingly, you reward him. In other words, demonstration, repetition and reward. Repeat the whole lesson, say three or four times to fix it in the dog's mind and then call it a day.

A dog is the only animal which will work for us willingly and at all times with no thought of reward other than a few kind words and a caress. Even these kind words, however, should be repetitive so that the dog is left in no doubt that he has pleased. 'Good dog, good dog, good dog'. These endearments should be accompanied by an abundance of pats and caresses. They should leave the dog in no doubt at all that he is a superb chap who has pleased us by his brilliance. He will be anxious to repeat the performance.

Conversely, the only correction he needs is a verbal one, 'Bad dog'. And really bark it out so that once again the dog is left in no doubt that he has displeased you. Praise and reward then is 'Good dog'; disapproval and correction 'Bad dog'.

'Sit'

'Sit'

You are ready to start the first lesson and as the simplest of all is 'Sit' it is suggested that you start with this.

Have the dog facing forward and on your left side. Hold the dog's lead high in the right hand to keep his head up, press the hind quarters to the ground with the left hand, repeating the one word 'Sit' all the time. As soon as he is in a sitting position reward him. After a minute or two, walk him round the room once again and then stop and repeat the routine. Demonstration, repetition and reward. Most dogs will learn to sit in a day or so; some in a few minutes, depending largely on their nature and how much they want to please you.

When the dog is sitting upon your instruction and without any pushing, you are nearly ready to take the next step and it should be noted that no progress can ever be made from one lesson to the next until the first is completely mastered. You should also remember that, like us, a dog likes to succeed. You should therefore always finish his lessons on a note of success. When, for example, he sits without pushing, it is better to call it a day, even a minute or two earlier than you had intended, rather than go on and finish with a few boring failures.

'Stay'

The next step is to try the same exercise without the lead. But as he is now without restraint you will have to work harder to hold his attention and be even more careful not to let the lesson go on too long. When he fully understands and obeys the instruction to sit both on and off the lead you proceed to the next lesson which is 'Stay'.

Back on the lead he goes, and back through the now familiar first routine. As he sits, however, you add the word 'Stay' and at the same time you hold his attention with an admonishing fore-finger and move out in front of him just the length of the lead. If he attempts to move his position you rap out 'Bad dog' and put him back into his original position.

A few sessions of this should teach him that 'Sit-Stay' means just that.

As all progress in training is a logical continuation it hardly needs saying that your next step is to ensure that the word 'Stay' is obeyed even when some distance separates you. As the lead is a constant reminder of your control over the dog, retain it but lengthen it by adding a few yards of light cord. Practise the 'stay' routine on the lead plus cord, first across the width of the room and later the length of the garden.

Next comes the 'stay' routine at a distance without the restraining cord and lead. This is a test for the trainer, and if you fail to hold your dog's attention and lose control at this juncture, you must go right back to the beginning of the training stint the next day.

Up to date in every case at the end of the 'stay' routine you must go back to him, stand on his right side, that is with him on your left where he started, pause a moment and then deliberately release him from his 'bondage'. The point of this is that he knows that 'Sit-Stay' means sit and stay until you tell him to get up again. If at this point he acquires the habit of sitting for a moment or two and then wandering towards you, you have both made backward progress!

'Come'

With the 'stay' perfected one can move on to the next and possibly most important lesson of all which is 'Come'. The majority of pet dogs seem to think they can come when it suits them! Unless a dog comes when called, whatever the temptations and distractions are, he is not trained. He is a danger to himself and others.

Back to the old routine. On the lead, long cord attached, 'Sit-Stay' instruction given, retreat the length of the lead, stand still for a moment and then introduce the following innovation:

Call out his name . . . 'Fido', then quickly add the command 'Come'. At the same time you pull him gently towards you with the lead, or rather the cord, encouraging him all the time and showing vast enthusiasm. When he reaches you, you really over-do the 'Good dogs' and the caresses. A few repeats. Break off.

At the next lesson you attempt to do it without the lead, in other words you leave him in a sitting free position, move yourself ten yards away, and on a deliberate and clear instruction; 'Fido-

Come', get him to trot towards you. As ever, the distance can be increased until he does it at a gallop from one end of the garden to the other.

To teach the recall this way is to take advantage of the dog's instinct. He dislikes being left in a sitting position when you are ten or twenty yards away. He dislikes sitting and he dislikes being left. By deliberately putting him in this exposed position you intensify his desire to come to you. When you give the command 'Come', he is more than willing to oblige.

Drive home this lesson of willing obedience in every way possible. By calling 'Come' when he is running to you anyway. Give him a 'Come' call from one room to another before you feed him or take him for a walk. Make it pleasant for him to come to you and make it an automatic reaction to the command.

'Walk to heel'

'Heel'

Now there only remains 'Heel' in the basic or elementary training. Put the dog on your left facing forward. Hold the lead in your right hand so that it crosses over your body, leaving the left hand free.

Step off smartly with the command 'forward'. If the dog moves in front of your knee, jerk him back into position sharply and rap out the word 'Heel'. When he is in the right place use your free left hand to caress him, but still keep on walking.

If he falls behind, urge him forward to the correct position by your voice and with encouraging movements of your left hand. Keep turning to right and left, turning about, and walking in a circle. Keep him interested and keep him on his toes.

It hardly needs saying that this training cannot be started in busy streets and parks because there are too many distractions. For a while this training should take place in your own garden.

It also hardly needs to be said that the next step is the same exercise off the lead. Then you will really have to concentrate. However, this will at least serve to remind you once again that lessons should never last too long. And the above serves the purpose of reminding one that even *this* lesson should not go on too long. The points have been made and when absorbed, can be applied to anything you wish to teach a dog. Even to sit up and beg or 'die for his country'!

All of the above applies to the overwhelming majority of dogs. It must be admitted, however, that there are some exceptions. Not as many as some owners think, but certainly some.

Owners who write to me saying 'My dog is perfect in every respect and obeys me in every way *except one*', are usually talking nonsense. If the dog is normal and absorbs most of what he is taught, the probability is that the instruction on the subject in question is at fault.

The exception is the neurotic, unbalanced, moronic or perhaps insane dog. This is unusual but not impossible. It happens with dogs just as it happens with humans.

Criminal and anti-social cases can be recovered but it is difficult work. Much better never to let them grow into this pattern of behaviour. And if you have the misfortune to inherit one when it is already set in its ways, my advice is to send it away to a professional trainer for a few weeks. And if *he* admits failure you should consider, not merely passing your problems on to somebody else, but whether a genuine misfit in society can ever find peace and happiness.

Nervous dogs are a different kettle of fish. There are thousands of them about. Not all of them have been 'manufactured'. Some are born that way. Experienced people can see them while they are still in the nest and they tend to avoid them knowing that the trait may well stay with them for life. Inexperienced people also spot them in the litter sometimes. But all too often they then feel sorry for them and protective towards them. They gather to their arms the wee misfits and give themselves, or rather buy themselves, a nice big problem to which there is usually no permanent solution.

But to say there is no solution is not to say the condition cannot be improved. It can. And the only effective method is a course of obedience training such as has been described earlier. Maybe it only gives the dogs sufficient confidence to cover up their nervousness. But this is at least a start. And there is evidence that it does more. By teaching them their place in the world it does give them a security and a genuine confidence which enable them to relax.

Finally we come to the comparatively few genuinely aggressive dogs. A lot of these have been manufactured by owners who either deliberately or unwittingly encourage it because they are secretly pleased by the fact that people fear their dogs. While no expert in human psychology it does seem to me that these people use their dogs to compensate for their own inability to impress the world.

A more common way of provoking aggression is to indulge in rough horse play with young puppies. Some breeds take to this with great glee. They use their strength, growl with much ferocity, indulge in little nips and sometimes seize an arm or leg firmly enough to hold if not to hurt.

This is a mistake. Dogs learn quickly. And once they have learned that they can inspire fear through the use of their teeth there is no telling if, when crossed, they may not put the question of who is really the boss to the test.

11 | Working Dogs

Even a book about family dogs should not ignore the fact that hundreds of thousands of dogs, both here and abroad, work for a living.

This is not new. Indeed it is almost as old as mankind. As mentioned in Chapter 2, the original partnership between man and dog grew up, not because there was a natural love between them but because they came to realize they were useful to each other. Man used dog to help his own ends. Dog used man because there were side benefits – in other words food and shelter. Affection came much later.

Most breeds were originally designed by man for a particular task. Some were guards; others hunters, beasts of burden, herders, truffle seekers, prayer wheel spinners and even flea traps. Over the centuries no job has proved impossible for the ever-versatile dog. Now, only four major tasks are left to him. Briefly they are security, herding, hunting and guide work.

I find guide work is the most interesting because although apparently simple, leading the blind is totally un-dog-like. With all other work man has merely encouraged and controlled the dog's natural instincts.

Take security. The desire to guard is instinctive in a dog. While still in the nest he practises it. And as a growing pup he takes over your home, using his eyes, ears and nose to protect it. The services and police have merely developed this natural characteristic. Sheepdogs are also doing what comes naturally. They *want* to chivvy sheep around. In truth, they really want to nip them but man has controlled that. He exploits the dog's urge to tangle with sheep and by skilful positioning moves the flock around.

All hunters are doing their own thing. The greyhound wants to chase. Pet gun dogs will willingly point a budgie in a cage! And Labradors have to be actively discouraged from retrieving unsuitable objects like waste paper baskets.

Guide dogs

A guide dog's work is totally different. No dog is born with a desire to lead a sightless man about. This has to be instilled. At the same time some things which do come naturally to a dog are eliminated.

He is taught to walk at man's speed, rather than at his natural trot. He learns to forget the joy of chasing cats; to stifle reaction to back-firing cars.

Instead of crossing roads at a sloping short cut, he must approach them at precise right angles. He stops at every kerb, and he never plays the natural game of beating a car by a well timed spurt. He has to consider obstacles which will affect his master. It is no longer enough to get himself under a low bough, he has to remember the height of his master's head. And he always has to allow clearance space for the bulk of a man on his left.

All this absorbed, the biggest lesson still remains. For thousands of years man has ordered and dog obeyed. Being pack animals, dogs accept this, they like having a boss. The guide dog lacks this prop, he has to take decisions and give orders. He, not man, decides when to stop and start, what to do and how to do it.

We see this work so often that we almost take it for granted. But it's still a minor miracle. The only example of an animal accepting final responsibility and giving instructions to man.

Security dogs

The second group of working dogs are what might be called the 'security group'. These embrace police dogs, army dogs, R.A.F. dogs, frontier dogs and even just plain guard dogs.

All of them are required to do rather different things and so all of them are trained in different ways. Basically the breeds used are Germanic in origin such as Alsatians, Rottweilers, Giant Schnauzers, Dobermanns and to a lesser extent, Boxers.

The army holds to the theory that every dog should be trained to a specialist role and used only in this way. This certainly has the advantage of being able to use breeds in which particular instincts are highly developed. Thus they use Labradors and Labrador crosses for tracking work. For plain guarding any big and aggressive dog is used. Border Collies and a variety of mongrels are used in mine detection, a relevant factor being that as they are lightweights they are likely to be able to indicate the whereabouts of a buried mine without setting it off. They also use messenger dogs which when released will return to their base like carrier pigeons! And medical dogs who search out wounded men and deliver urgent supplies to them.

The Royal Air Force approach is different, principally because their requirements are different. Basically the R.A.F. merely require that their airfields be kept free of intruders regardless of whether they are enemy saboteurs or potential riflers of the canteen cigarettes. So first they use the only breed which is of itself a deterrent. The Alsatian, a dog recognized and respected anywhere in the world. Next, far from being secretive about the presence of dogs on the airfield, they willingly advertise the fact. They just want the 'baddies' to stay away.

Since the dogs always stay inside the airfield perimeter all dogs are trained to do all necessary tasks. Clearly finding wounded, long-range tracking, message carrying etc., are not required. But what they must be able to do is scent a man without fail, go into attack even in the face of gunfire, surmount any obstacles, guard prisoners and only attack if escape seems likely, give warning of approach of strangers and stand up to any weather. Most are savage brutes but they do their job.

Police requirements are different again. They really need an all-purpose dog but one which is basically gentle and kindly. They spend 90% of their time amongst law abiding members of the general public and a tendency to bite would soon be criticized. Nevertheless they also may have to attack in the face of gunfire so they must not be soft.

Generally the police demand and receive the best dogs. They even breed them to ensure they combine all the best qualities plus the required physical robustness necessary.

Herding dogs

In the past many breeds were used for particular herding tasks. For example the Old English Sheepdog for driving cattle to market, the Rough Collie for pure herding in the Scottish Highlands and the Corgi for driving cattle to and from the pastures in rural Wales.

Now because of their uncanny aptitude for the task, the Border Collie is employed to the virtual exclusion of all other breeds. Centuries ago farmers realized that with a dog they could control sheep far more easily. Dividing a flock and driving them into four different fields could take a man hours, a dog minutes.

They therefore learned to control dogs and in the Border found a willing pupil. All of the Border's instinct is concentrated on returning stragglers to the flock. This instinct is no mere happy accident but the result of generations of selective breeding.

Those bitches and dogs which gambolled round the flocks barking gaily were ruthlessly eliminated, at least from the breeding programmes. Pups which did not show an instinct to work sheep as soon as they left the nest were found 'good', i.e. pet homes. In time the breed's knowledge of both shepherds and sheep has become a part of them. They know that upon stopping they must always turn in towards the sheep and that they can control sheep with their hard unblinking stare.

Farmers know the spectacular worker is not always the best. A slow guide towards the flock is better than a barking dash which canters the sheep in a series of zig-zags, thereby running valuable weight off them. A dog who drops too frequently is frowned upon. He loses momentum and therefore wastes time. But the most important single thing is that a dog, having been sent to a certain position in the field must divine what is wanted of him then, and work on his own initiative until given further commands.

Gundogs

Many thousands of gundogs are still used regularly in this country and abroad. There are three different types of work available to them. First there are those breeds which work alongside the sportsman, driving game out of cover so that it can be shot. Many of them will then also retrieve it on command. The breeds most commonly used for this are the Spaniels and principally the Cocker and English Springer.

Next come those dogs who work well out in front of the guns in open country such as on moors. These are the Pointers and Setters and their task is to quarter the ground from right to left, left to right until they get a scent of game. Then they freeze, one paw held aloft, tail straight out behind, nose pointing towards the find. The sportsman, having been alerted goes up to the dog and both creep forward until the birds lose their nerve and break cover. A bang, and it is all over.

Finally there are the Retrievers, pure specialists bred for one task only; that of bringing back shot game from well nigh impossible positions. They climb banks, swim streams, wade into marshy or boggy ground; and when a bird has only been injured, perhaps in the wing, they gallop after it and bring it back without harming a feather on its head.

The one thing that all the dogs above have in common, be they herders, security dogs, gundogs or guides is a quick and certain response to orders. Their training varies in countless different ways. But it all starts from the same simple beginnings. Before they can be taught any of their specialized roles they must learn to Sit, Stay, Heel and Come. And what is good enough for the world's most advanced canine specialists is also good enough for the average pet dog in the average family home.

12 | Breeding

Perhaps the first thing you should know about breeding dogs is that there is no necessity to do it if you don't want to.

Usually the case is put like this: 'I have a three-year-old pedigree bitch and I realize she should have puppies'. Then the complications such as insufficient space, lack of experience, long absences from the house etc., are mentioned before: 'I know she must have one litter but how can it be done?'

My answer is 'Don't even try'. And further to demolish the myth that every bitch should have one litter. From a health point of view there is no reason why bitches should have puppies. True, some who don't have minor internal complications later in life. But so do just as many who do. And either way, a relatively simple operation corrects the position.

True, most bitches get pleasure from rearing pups. It matures them and makes them better pets. They frequently become more confident, loyal and home-loving, but against these possible advantages must be set the drawbacks. One of these is that the operation is time consuming, and some people are just too busy to make the sacrifice. Good intentions alone are no help once the puppies are born because they and their mother want frequent and considerable attention.

When this stage has passed, there comes the problem of selling the pups which can prove more difficult than it sounds. You might be left with, say, eight lusty pups on your hands. The result is something close to panic. You can see the planned profit disappearing at every meal time. Young puppies have enormous and costly appetites.

The disadvantages are easy to see if you approach the proposition with your eyes open. The advantages, although just as real are harder to pin down. Thousands of people undertake it every week because they know it will bring them pleasure. They enjoy looking after 'mum', they work willingly for the pups, they mix food, clean up mess, pay vets' bills, work and worry over every single pup.

The experienced know they are unlikely to show a profit, but they still do it for love. If you are that sort of person, and if you have the time, then I would be the last to suggest you should not breed an occasional litter. And the decision to do this will almost certainly start you worrying about inbreeding. So let's have a look at that bogy and maybe demolish another myth.

Nowadays most real or imaginary faults in pedigree dogs are blamed on so called inbreeding. 'Is my Poodle disobedient because he is too inbred?' 'Is it inbreeding which makes my Peke a fussy feeder?' 'Would inbreeding cause canker in my Cocker's ears?' The answer is 'No' in every case. Dogs are disobedient because they have not been trained; fussy feeders because they have been taught to be and they have canker because their ears are not clean.

In each case it is the owner who has spoiled the dog but the breeder who gets the blame. Moreover, in ninety-nine cases out of a hundred, when dog owners put the blame on inbreeding an examination of the pedigree shows that it has never taken place!

Inbreeding is the mating of closely related animals, such as sire to daughter, son to mother or even brother to sister. Why is it ever practised? Simply because it's a short cut to fixing family likenesses. It enables breeders to concentrate the desirable features and pack them into the offspring. Unfortunately, it also fixes undesirable features in the same way, which is why breeders in fact very rarely resort to it.

Among human beings, where the survival of the fittest does not apply, close mating is taboo. With the lower animals, however, particularly in the wild state, what could be more natural than that they, the dogs, horses or even lions, should mate those animals they are in everyday contact with despite the fact that they are often *very* closely related. Inevitably a proportion of the offspring, being defective, fail to survive.

Man, then, has not introduced inbreeding. Rather, by domesticating certain animals he now controls it. Neither for that matter has he been able to alter the simple fact that inbreeding is not creative. It adds nothing. It merely fixes and accentuates what is already there.

So if you are inexperienced you might be wise to avoid genuine inbreeding. But equally you would be wise to adopt line breeding, that is the breeding of animals from the same line or strain. At its simplest this is achieved merely by using animals which have one or more of the same ancestral names in their pedigrees.

There is no point in enlarging on this theme here. Nor can the principles of genetics be properly explored. Those pet owners who decide to become serious breeders must read one of the many excellent books on these subjects when they have the opportunity to consider all aspects of what are large, complicated and even controversial subjects.

The fact that breeding often improves a bitch's temperament as mentioned earlier does not mean that sexual experience improves a male dog; indeed it often has the reverse effect. A pet dog which is mated to a bitch gets no lasting pleasure. He does not reap the same emotional harvest as the bitch who brings up and enjoys the litter. His is but a fleeting satisfaction and, far from quieting his sexual instincts, it stimulates them. He has had one success; why not another if he searches diligently enough?

The bitch's season

But to return to the bitch. She will normally come into season at between six and twelve months of age, and thereafter at about six monthly intervals for the remainder of her life. The period of season usually lasts some three weeks and is accompanied by a slightly stained discharge and a swelling of the sexual organ.

During this time she will become restless about the house because the urge to mate is strong within her. She can, unfortunately, no longer be trusted not to run away. Indeed nature forces her to attempt this. She must therefore be exercised only on the lead, no matter how obedient she may be normally. Additionally, it is folly to turn her out in the garden to take exercise. The discharge carries with it a strong scent which is unnoticeable to us but very attractive to male admirers. Some may be sitting about outside the house, which means that even if she does not jump out of the garden to meet them, one will jump in to mate her!

Should you decide to breed a litter it is often better to enlist the aid of a stud dog from a recognized kennel, because it is better value. The dog in question will be a winner at shows, making the puppies potentially more valuable. Additionally, the owner will have the necessary experience to effect the mating – something which is often much more difficult than it sounds. The ideal time is generally thought to be on the twelfth day after the season starts. Often, however, the season has remained unnoticed by pet owners for a few days because the coloured discharge has not commenced. This means that the eighth or ninth known day is more likely to be correct.

When the bitch is ready for service it is immediately apparent, not only will she 'stand' for any dog but if you touch her back she will curl her tail to one side.

Pregnancy

The bitch carries the puppies for approximately sixty-three days – that is nine weeks. If she has been maintained on a proper diet there is no reason to alter this at the beginning of her pregnancy. Equal parts by weight of dog meal and dog meat make an adequate ration for the gestating bitch. If the bitch has previously had trouble in rearing puppies, however, the introduction of a vitamin mineral preparation should be considered. Perhaps even more important in this case is that consideration should be given to the advisability of breeding from her at all.

During the fifth week, or sometimes a little earlier, her appetite will increase and she must be given more food. The amount depends in part on the size of the litter. By the eighth week a bitch carrying a normal litter may be eating nearly twice as much food as usual. This is too much food for one meal a day, so the total must be broken up into two or three parts. She will also be thirsty, and milk, up to a pint a day for medium sized breeds, should be given.

In the ninth week, food intake usually falls, although the bitch continues to be thirsty. During and immediately after whelping, water or milk must be freely available.

During her period of pregnancy she should pay at least one visit to the veterinary surgeon for examination and he should be advised of the likely date of whelping. Whether or not a veterinary surgeon needs to be present depends entirely on the circumstances.

Whelping

A bitch normally whelps easily and without outside aid. She knows by instinct how to open the bag which surrounds the new born pup, how to sever the cord, to stimulate the whelp into breathing by her tongue, to free its nose and mouth of mucus so that it can breathe, to nuzzle it towards her teats for food and to relax to await the birth of the next one.

This is the normal course of events. Sometimes, however, there are complications, some of which are serious. There is no point in detailing them here because if they occur you want skilled attention at the earliest opportunity; this is the point of giving the veterinary surgeon prior warning.

Within a day of whelping the bitch should have regained her appetite. The amount of extra food required depends on the number and weight of the litter. For example, one Miniature Poodle successfully reared a litter of eight, but her food consumption rose to three large tins of Top Dog a day – over three times her usual ration.

A bitch's milk contains up to three times as much protein as cows' milk. She supplies rich protein food at such a rate that a

litter at weaning often weighs as much as the bitch herself. It follows that her demand for protein is enormous and the simplest way to meet it is to increase substantially the meat she is given, while keeping the biscuit ration to the normal maintenance level. Milk, which contains both protein and calcium should also be given. This large amount of food must necessarily be divided into several meals.

Her diet should also contain sufficient calcium and phosphorus in an easily assimilable form. A puppy grows by laying down body tissues consisting mainly of protein and water and by developing its bones. Bones contain much calcium and phosphorus, which the puppy gets direct from its mother. The mother must obtain them from her diet and milk is an excellent source. True, it makes the bitch loose, but this is preferable to risking Eclampsia, an often fatal condition resulting from the bitch's resources of available calcium being overtaxed by the demands on her.

In those breeds which have their tails docked, such as Fox Terriers and Poodles, a veterinary surgeon should be asked to perform this service when the pups are three or four days old. There is no hardship or lasting discomfort about this and indeed most whelps are playing happily again two or three minutes after the operation. At the same time, those useless appendages – the dew claws – may be removed.

For the first three weeks the bitch does everything that is necessary for the pups. This includes not merely feeding them but cleaning and exercising them. Their eyes open on about the tenth day, after which they sometimes become a little more venturesome, often straying a foot or so away from their mother but rarely beyond the confines of the whelping pen.

Weaning

Weaning time is fast approaching. But before discussing it in detail we consider the basic nutritional requirements of the puppy to ensure normal growth and development.

A puppy's needs are the same in character as an adult dog's. Water, protein, fat, vitamins, minerals, roughage and energy (Calories) must be supplied by the diet. But, as a thriving pup doubles its birthweight in less than a week and continues to gain its birthweight about every five days up to five or six months, special requirements occur. To achieve this growth pups must eat much more than an adult of the same weight and its calorie intake must be higher to provide both growth and maintenance. The increased needs for other nutrients are almost directly proportional to this increased calorie intake. Therefore a weaned puppy can be fed a diet nutritionally balanced for an adult dog and obtain the extra nutrients for growth simply by eating more. The nutrients particularly important are protein and minerals to build muscle, organs and bones; and the vitamins, notably A and D. But before the pup can be fed a balanced diet it must be weaned from the exclusive diet of its mother's milk.

The weaning age depends mainly on the progress made by the litter and the mother's behaviour. Usually sharp teeth begin to appear during the third week which hurts the dam. This is aggravated by scratching with ever lengthening claws.

Left to herself, the mother would probably regurgitate partially digested food for her litter. Her milk would fade, then dry and the pups would learn to share their mother's food. They would also learn to lap water. This natural weaning is not satisfactory for practical dog breeding as a domestic environment destroys the natural instincts or behaviour patterns. A greedy mother may refuse to allow the pups near any food. Some pups may fall behind although they have survived during lactation when receiving adequate maternal care. Natural weaning frequently leads to heavy mortality and irregular growth.

Methods adopted to replace the natural process vary widely but all attempt to effect the transition from mother's milk to the new dietary regime with the minimum disturbance to the puppies' rate of growth and development. When weaning is complete, the litter should be gaining weight at least as fast as during lactation.

For such successful weaning certain conditions must be met:

1. The weaning food must be palatable enough to attract the pups.
2. It must have physical properties which allow chewing by very young pups.

3. It must be nutritionally balanced to allow optimum growth and development.
4. The diet must suit the pups' digestive processes.
5. Kennel management must provide a suitable environment for the pups, both as a litter and individually.

In meeting these conditions, dog breeders have devised a remarkable range of methods employing many different types of food. The two most popular methods are those which start by introducing semi-solid food, and those which start the puppies lapping milk or a milk-based liquid. The latter are less laborious and consequently more common.

Usually weaning is begun when the litter is three weeks old. The pups are put beside a saucer of warm cows' milk and encouraged to lap by offering a milk-covered finger for licking and then by putting their muzzles in the milk. This procedure should be carried out three or four times a day at what will become regular meal-times; breakfast, midday and evening. In the main alternative method the pups are first offered small amounts of raw beef which has been scraped to form a paste.

There is no need to feed a healthy weaned puppy more frequently than three times a day. Controlled tests have shown that the puppy's stomach, regardless of breed size, is large enough to ingest sufficient of a balanced diet twice a day to support optimum growth. A third meal, of milk alone, should be given at midday until the puppy is about two months old and fully adjusted to its new dietary regime.

Returning to weaning, puppies should be lapping greedily within a few days and reduction of the mother's diet can begin. The next stage is to add some form of cereal to the milk. Proprietary baby foods such as Farex and Farlene are useful and are stirred into hot milk to give a gruel or thick soup. A nutritionally balanced puppy meal in pellet or granule form which soaks up boiling milk is even better. The mixture is cooled to blood heat before feeding. Suitable proportions are equal parts by volume of meal and milk, this being equivalent to rather more than twice as much milk as meal by weight. It should be offered twice a day, morning and evening, milk only being given at midday. The protein content of the puppy meal should be about

20% and it should be fortified with a vitamin/mineral supplement.

At first the pups try to drink or suck any unabsorbed milk but each day the quantity of solid food taken increases. The dam is now removed for long periods but drinking water must always be available to the pups. After a few days the puppies should be accepting the food readily and the mother can be removed except at night. By the time the litter is six weeks old, and often sooner, weaning is complete. The mother's milk should have dried up, her food intake having been reduced to the normal maintenance level, and she can be removed altogether. Meanwhile the solid content of the pups' diet has been increased by adding more meal to the milk, or by introducing in moderation a little scraped beef, or other form of meat. Some breeders favour one, or more usually two, meals a day based on meat and one or two based on cereal food plus milk. There is no scientific evidence to suggest any benefit from varying the diet in this way, provided that a balanced diet is given each day.

Owing to the variation in size and the difference in development rates it is difficult to be precise about the quantities six-week-old pups should be consuming. However the following table gives average figures for the daily intake of three popular breeds.

Average Daily Food Consumption of 6-week-old Puppies

Breed	Weight of Pup lb	METHOD 1		METHOD 2		
		Puppy Meal	Milk	Scraped Beef	Baby Cereal	Milk
		oz	pint	oz	oz	pint
Labrador	8	3½	1	4	2	¾
Beagle	5½	2½	½	2¾	1½	½
Min. Poodle	3	1½	¼	1½	1	¼

These amounts should be divided between two main meals, with some milk being reserved for a midday drink.

As a check on progress weigh the pups individually once or twice a week on household scales calibrated in ½-oz divisions.

The rate of gain should be regular. It depends mostly on breed size and individual nature. Very roughly, Miniature Poodles gain 1 oz, Beagles 2 oz and Labradors 4 oz a day from weaning to five or six months of age.

Difficulties rarely arise during weaning which cannot be resolved by patience and special attention to individual puppies. Sometimes a bitch, particularly if the litter is small, has provided so well that the satiated puppies are reluctant even to try to lap. Reducing the mother's food decreases the milk flow and heightens the puppies' interest in what you provide! Other pups accept semi-solid food, such as scraped beef, more readily than milk, but if the bitch is happy and fit, weaning can be delayed for a week or more without harm.

Should the puppies become listless, appear out of condition, vomit frequently or be excessively loose for more than one day, veterinary advice must be obtained.

By the time the pups are six weeks old, each should be receiving two main meals a day, based on cereal and milk, and probably some meat, with a third milk feed at midday. Puppies should be fed individually or in pairs from now on to ensure fair shares and weekly weighing should continue.

It is possible to rear dogs successfully on an exclusive diet of one of the nutritionally complete dry meals now available, but for the vast majority, meat is still an important part of the diet. Almost any form of meat can now be introduced, if not already present, at one or both of the main meals. The meat, preferably cooked to avoid bacterial infection and parasite eggs, should be given in moderation at first. Liver is a laxative and should not be given alone to young puppies. Tinned dog meats are eminently suitable, again in moderation at first, and have the advantages of convenience, sterility and (usually) fortification with a balanced vitamin/mineral supplement. Boned fish is also satisfactory, as are cooked eggs. Whatever meat is given it should be minced and mixed with cereal and the milk can be added or given separately.

An integral part of the weaning process is worming to prevent roundworms obtaining a hold. This is best done by administering a piperazine preparation obtainable at most chemists, at 3, 5½ and 8 weeks in accordance with the instructions on the packet. If in doubt consult a veterinarian.

All you have to do now is sell the puppies! And here conditions and circumstances vary so much that no useful advice can be given. Two points can however be made. First that pet owners cannot expect to receive quite the same price as that obtained by commercial breeding kennels – the latter have usually spent many years and large sums on perfecting their 'marketing arrangements' – you are unknown.

The other point is that pet owners should rarely, perhaps never, keep puppies to ensure getting top prices. At eight weeks a pup is at its most attractive; it is also becoming its hungriest, and a few more weeks could make it less saleable – and far less profitable.

Before leaving this chapter a reminder that some pups are born orphans. As an appendix to this book is given a tried and trusted method of hand rearing them. It is to be hoped that you never have to refer to it!

13 | Dog Shows

Mention the words 'dog show' anywhere in Britain and almost immediately comes the response: 'Cruft's'. It is the one show everybody has heard of. To many, it is the only show which exists. Which means that it comes as a shock to learn that there are over 2,000 official dog shows of various sizes held in the British Isles every year; and they have been going on for over 100 years.

The first dog show in Britain, which incidentally was the first in the world, took place at Newcastle on 29th June 1859, and was restricted to Setters and Pointers. It consisted of one class of each and was not an event which excited great comment in the outside world.

However, it seems to have been sufficiently interesting to have captured the imagination of some enterprising people in Birmingham, because a show was held there in November of the same year and, from that date, shows of a far less restricted nature became a regular feature in that city. As time passed, enthusiasts in other towns tried their hands at the same thing with varying degrees of success.

It is possible that the happy advent of that organizing genius, Mr. Charles Cruft, saved the idea of dog shows from fading away, for although some thirty years had elapsed since the first event at Newcastle, he took a serious hand in the pastime, and shows took on an entirely new look under his guidance. He was a man blessed with enormous enthusiasm and a natural flair for knowing what the public wanted a little before they knew it themselves! In other words he was a showman.

At fourteen years of age Charles Cruft joined James Spratt (later Spratts Patent Ltd. and now a member of the Spillers

5

group of companies) in a business venture concerned with the
then revolutionary idea of manufacturing biscuits for dogs. As a
traveller he was a success, and before many years he was
travelling the continent and obtaining orders from dog breeders
there. The Paris Exhibition of 1878 started him on his life work,
when some of the breeders in France asked him to arrange a
canine section for this great event. His flair for organization soon
became apparent. He first staged his own show in 1886 at the
old Royal Aquarium in London, moved it to the Royal
Agricultural Hall in 1891, and continued to run it there as an
annual event until his death at the age of eighty-six in 1938.

During these early years, a governing body grew up in the
United Kingdom, under the title of the Kennel Club, beginning

in 1873 with the banding together of a number of interested men under the guidance of the late Mr. S. E. Shirley, M.P. One of its first tasks was that of framing the rules for Dog Shows.

Skipping the intervening years, we can move straight to the present day with the statement that there are now four types of shows in Britain. Three of them are official, that is the Sanction, Open and Championship: the other, that is the Exemption show, might be called 'semi official' because it has the blessing of the Kennel Club but no official status. Exemption shows are dealt with first, not because they are the most important, indeed the reverse is true, but because they are the type at which the majority of pet owners first become acquainted with the pastime.

Exemption shows are so called because upon request being made, the Kennel Club grants them exemption from the otherwise strict rule that only dogs registered with the Kennel Club may compete. Therefore you can enter 'Bob' or 'Bess' without red tape or formality. This is just as well as these shows are normally held on village greens and in conjunction with village fetes, gymkhanas etc., where formality is unknown!

The shows are usually divided into about a dozen classes, of which four are restricted to pedigree dogs only. These might be for Puppies, Sporting Dogs, Terriers or Veterans. Additionally, there are usually eight or so 'fun' classes where entrants can be either pure or cross-bred with prizes for the Waggiest Tail, Most Soulful Eyes, Best Condition and so on.

The whole thing is meant to be fun and it usually is. These shows have no great significance except that they provide a day out for ordinary pet owners and serve as an introduction to the rather more exacting and rewarding official shows.

As mentioned earlier, these are of three types, the Sanction, Open and Championship.

Sanction shows

The Sanction shows are by far the most numerous and could be described as the nursery, both for exhibits and exhibitors. Sanction shows are usually restricted to twenty classes, are open only to members of the organizing club, which in practice means that the entry is likely to be drawn from a comparatively small

5*

radius, and the quality of the competition is controlled by a rule which forbids the exhibition of champions or near champions. Further, the classes are graded, 'handicapped' as it were, so that well-known dogs which have won many times are barred from all but the top few classes. This, then, is the type of show at which you should make your debut.

Open shows

The second class of show, the Open show is, as its name implies, open to all, and not restricted to members of the organizing club. Here the total number of classes for all breeds may be anything from thirty-five to three or four hundred. Naturally the competition is keener, and the standard of the exhibits somewhat higher.

Championship shows

Finally, there are the Championship shows and, as these are run on a nationwide basis, we may expect to see at them the best dogs in the land. At these shows, Kennel Club Challenge Certificates are awarded to the dog and the bitch respectively which the judge considers the best of breed. As there may be anything up to one hundred or more of each sex entered, it is no easy task to win this certificate – which is in effect a statement signed by the judge that he considers the chosen exhibit worthy of the title of champion. This does not make the dog a champion, however, as this premier award must be won under three different judges before the owner may put the magic word 'Champion' before the dog's name.

Classification

The sexes are normally divided; that is there are classes for dogs and classes for bitches. A typical example of the classification is given below. It should be noted that each of the nine classes is duplicated for both dogs and bitches.

Puppy: For dogs and bitches of six and not exceeding twelve calendar months of age.

Maiden: For dogs and bitches which have not won a first prize of the value of £1 or more.

Novice: For dogs and bitches which have not won more than two first prizes, each of the value of £1 or more.

Undergraduate: For dogs and bitches which have not won more than two first prizes, each of the value of £2 or more.

Note: No dog is eligible for entry in Maiden, Novice or Undergraduate classes which has won a challenge certificate or has obtained any award that counts towards the title of Champion under the rules of any governing body recognized by the Kennel Club.

Post Graduate: For dogs and bitches which have not won more than four first prizes of the value of £2 or more in Post Graduate, Minor Limit, Mid-Limit, Limit or Open classes.

Minor Limit: For dogs and bitches which have not won two Challenge Certificates or more than two first prizes in all, each of the value of £2 or more.

Mid-Limit: For dogs and bitches which have not won three challenge certificates or more than four first prizes in all, each of the value of £2 or more, in Open, Limit and Mid-Limit classes.

Limit: For dogs and bitches which have not won three Challenge Certificates under three different judges, or more than six first prizes in all, each of the value of £2 or more, in Open or Limit classes.

Open: For all dogs and bitches.

Rules and regulations for the beginner

The actual mechanics of entering your dog for a show are very simple. Keep watch on the advertisements in the dog papers (*Our Dogs* and *Dog World*, both published weekly) until you find a show taking place in your district. The secretary of the show concerned will, on request, send you a schedule of the show and an entry form. No dog may be entered at a show until it has been registered with the Kennel Club, and if your dog is not already registered you must apply to the Secretary of the Kennel Club, at 1 Clarges Street, Piccadilly, London W1Y 8AB, for a registration form, which is provided free. Having chosen the name of the dog, return the form to the K.C. with the registration fee.

You then select the classes in which you wish to enter your dog to compete, and enter them on the form which should be returned to the secretary of the organizing club. You are required to sign the following declaration on the bottom of the entry form:

'I undertake to abide by the Rules and Regulations of the Kennel Club and of this show and I declare that the dogs entered have not suffered from or been knowingly exposed to the risk of distemper or any contagious disease including any reaction to immunization during the six weeks prior to exhibition and I will not show them if they incur such risks between now and the day of the show or if they have been immunized within fourteen days prior to the show.

'I declare that to the best of my knowledge the dogs are not liable to disqualification under Kennel Club Show Regulations.'

Apart from its strict intention, this declaration will serve the useful purpose of reminding you that before and after visiting a show you should take full precautions against your dog contracting an infectious disease. Veterinary inspections are no longer obligatory, and in any case they were of little avail against a dog which had contracted a disease but not yet manifested symptoms of it.

A golden rule is never to take a dog to a show which is a bit off colour, not only because he is unlikely to do well unless he is quite fit, nor entirely for the protection of your fellow exhibitors, but because a dog which is not at its best is far more likely to contract disease than one which is fit.

When you arrive at the show, the dog must usually be benched under its number, so that visitors may look at the dogs and identify them with the numbers in their catalogues. If, however, it is a small, unbenched show, the dog may stay with you all the time whether you are in the ring or not. You are responsible for presenting your dog at the ringside in time for it to be judged in the classes entered. All that remains to be done then, is for the judge to examine your dog, place him in his order of merit in relation to the other exhibits and award the prizes.

No book can teach you the art of presenting and preparing your dog to the best advantage, and no amount of reading will teach you the art of handling a dog in the ring. The only school in which you can learn these all important lessons is the one named 'Experience'.

You can help your dog on the day by careful training in deportment beforehand. He should be taught from an early age to let strangers handle and examine him. Then he should be taught to walk properly and to stand naturally at the end of this walk.

Inducements may be used to make him take an interest in the proceedings by, for example, holding a piece of cooked liver in your hand. When he knows the lessons perfectly, put yourself in the position of a judge in the middle of a ring and let somebody else walk the dog in circles round you. This should tell you exactly what pace, hold, etc., best suits the dog and so enables you to present him to the best advantage.

If you are showing a small dog you will be asked to put him on a table for the judge's examination and this is something to which he should be thoroughly accustomed before the day of the show.

All of this, however, will avail you little unless your dog is shown in the peak of his physical condition. Only with the bloom of health upon him can he hope to do justice to himself. Physical perfection can only be brought about by good food, fresh air, adequate exercise (of which a large proportion should be given on hard roads on a lead), daily grooming over a long period, and the mental well-being which is inseparable from a happy and contented disposition.

He should also be a good dog!

14 | Administration and the Law

Maybe this is not a very good title for a chapter, but it's the best all-embracing one I can think of. It would, however, be unfortunate if it conveyed the impression that there's a lot of 'paper work' to be done in order to become and remain a dog owner. Fortunately there's little risk of that. It must already be widely known that all you *have* to do in the way of office work to become a dog owner is sign the cheque and pass it over to the seller, which is easy enough and only mildly painful!

Leaving aside this minimum, there is quite a lot which the conscientious dog owner will want to know, perhaps more than one chapter like this can possibly tell. This will, however, at least serve as an introduction, permitting the reader to explore more fully if so minded.

The law

The law has been changed quite drastically recently by virtue of the Animals Bill which reached the Statute Book in October 1971.

Oddly enough it excited comparatively little comment for a far-reaching piece of legislation which put far greater responsibility on to animal owners than they had ever experienced before. It made them liable for damage done to any other person or his property. It removed from them the immunity which they had previously enjoyed from accepting financial responsibility for their pets' misdeeds.

For example, now if your straying pet causes a traffic accident you are legally liable and it is no defence to say that you did not know your dog was out. You may think the financial risks are slight but straying dogs are said to cause accidents in which 450 people are killed annually. Until this Act became law, the victims had no effective legal remedy against animal owners. Now they have. Equally immune in the past were the owners of animals said to have caused some 2,500 traffic accidents in one recent year alone. Admittedly these figures must be accepted with some reserve. Some motorists are not above inventing a mythical dog to explain away human error; but even allowing for this, the number of traffic accidents caused by dogs must be disconcertingly high.

Imagine the bill for damages if Fido's roaming caused the death of a magnate and the wreckage of his Rolls Royce. Clearly the owners most at risk are those living in towns or near busy roads. It is they who must now take even more stringent precautions.

Another section of the Bill deals with dangerous animals and it is mentioned here because the dog could, under certain circumstances, be numbered amongst them. These characters come under two headings. First there are the dangerous species such as lions, tigers, snakes and other zoo-type beasts which need not concern us. Next there are the animals which although normally docile and tractable can, and sometimes do, display 'dangerous characteristics'. This must include dogs. If you have one which is known to bite, watch out. Even if you only think it might, it is still your responsibility to ensure no person is ever bitten. And the fallacy of the dog being allowed one 'free' bite is now even more fallacious than it was before.

Guard dogs are in a different category. If one bites a burglar it would probably be considered reasonable by the courts as he was protecting property and premises. But were he to bite a lawful and legitimate caller such as the postman, tradesman or a friend, the defence that he was a 'guard dog' would not avail you. The question of insurance against this risk is discussed later.

This Act apart, the dog has always been the only domestic animal against whom tax is levied and the only household pet with legal rights and liabilities for his owner.

Licences

He is required to be licensed after he reaches six months of age, the annual fee being 37½p. To be more precise the owner is licensed to keep a dog, from which it follows that licences are not transferable. The owner is defined as the person on whose premises the dog lives, which clearly means that if you take in a stray, you become the owner and need a licence. The penalty for keeping a dog without a licence or for having more dogs than are licensed is a fine of £5. There is a similar penalty for refusing to produce this licence on demand by a police constable or other authorized person.

There are no all-in breeders' licences and if a litter is kept after it is six months of age, all must be licensed. The only exceptions granted are for guide dogs for blind persons, dogs used solely for shepherding or cattle droving and certain hounds owned by bona fide hunting packs.

All dogs on the highway, whether on the lead or not, must wear a metal plate or disc bearing the owner's name and address. This regrettably is more honoured in the breach than the observance, but it is still the law and can be enforced. It is also a sensible precaution.

Restrictions

In certain designated areas, principally urban districts, it is an offence to permit any dog to be in the streets at any time, whether alone or accompanied, unless he is on a lead.

Although it is not correct that a dog may be shot by a landowner for trespass, farmers and stock breeders do have considerable protection. They are allowed to shoot if they believe that the life of their stock is imperilled.

This can be interpreted rather freely. A farmer, seeing a dog dashing towards his sheep, might shoot first and ask questions afterwards. It would be difficult to prove he did not think a destructive attack was imminent.

Magistrates can order a dog deemed dangerous to be kept under control. Fines of £1 per day can be levied if this order is not complied with. Magistrates can also order dangerous dogs to be destroyed.

Dogs fouling pavements can be dealt with by the law by fines on their owners. Many, including myself, feel that this deterrent is not sufficiently used.

Quarantine

Quarantine regulations are widely known and equally widely resented and disliked! Even so, they are designed for our and our dogs' protection. The object is to keep rabies, one of the most dreadful diseases known to mankind, away from these shores. The disease, spread only by direct contact with an infected animal or person can incubate for up to six months without any signs being shown. When symptoms develop, however, death is inevitable and follows within three to five days.

Certain other countries which have rabies in their natural wild-life must do the best they can to reduce the risk of its spread by inoculations. These are good but not 100% effective. Quarantine is. So every dog coming from abroad has to spend six months at its owner's expense in a registered quarantine kennel under the supervision of a veterinary surgeon. The penalty for smuggling, or attempted smuggling, is high and usually includes confiscation of the animal. The risks to life in this country are even higher!

Registration

Now to more cheerful subjects! Principally the registration of dogs with the Kennel Club. Any pure bred dog born from registered parents is automatically eligible for registration. Application for a registration form, supplied free, should be made to the Kennel Club, 1 Clarges Street, Piccadilly, London W1Y 8AB.

On it must be entered the date of birth, name of parents and the chosen name for the dog, after which it must be returned with the registration fee ruling at the time. In due course details will be published in the *Kennel Gazette* and no other dog will ever be permitted to use this name.

This is a double-edged weapon. It means that you cannot use the name of any other registered dog. Since nearly 200,000 are registered a year, say nearly a million in the last six years alone, your choice is rather restricted. Bob, Bess and Bambi are clearly out!

The breeders' way out of this is to take out a prefix or 'trade name', for example 'Willwin'. Then he can call his pups Willwin Bob, Bess and Bambi without trouble. But even finding a prefix which has not been used before is much more difficult than it sounds.

When a registered dog is sold, it is usual for the seller to give with it a signed transfer form, which is completed by the buyer and forwarded to the Kennel Club with, once again, a small fee. This enables the transfer to be recorded.

Pedigree form

None of the above should be confused with a pedigree form. This latter is entirely unofficial and is merely a list of the parents and ancestors of the puppy concerned, prepared and usually signed by the breeder. Whilst it is useful to have as a record, it has no real value other than to enable the owner to identify and therefore register the dog with the Kennel Club *if* both its parents were registered. I realize that this statement will not stop countless thousands of owners from treasuring 'Percy's' pedigree and guarding it like the Crown Jewels!

Insurance

Insurance is a subject which should at least be considered in this chapter. Briefly this is of two types. Firstly, insurance to protect yourself – that is first party insurance. Next third party insurance, that is to protect others, or to be more precise to protect you against claims made by others for damage or loss which your dog may cause.

Clearly under the latter heading must come claims arising from the afore-mentioned Animals Bill 1971. A word of warning here: if claims are made against you they are likely to be very large and the cost of litigation could swell them to astronomical proportions. If cover is to be obtained, therefore, it must be very substantial, preferably unlimited, and it must be backed by companies of the highest repute and so worded as to obviate any risk of the liability being repudiated on any grounds.

The best advice therefore is that if you are considering third party insurance you should consult a reputable insurance broker and ask him to negotiate an agreement, preferably through Lloyds, which will hold water in the event of disaster. Anything else will leave you in a fool's paradise until precisely the moment you need real help.

The other type of insurance has always seemed to me of doubtful value: that is the insuring of a dog for its alleged value. Some may find payment of say £25 if 'Spot' is run over of some consolation, but I suspect the number is few. In any case 'Spot' has no real value; as a saleable object he is valueless and you might have trouble giving him away. As a treasured possession, however, he might be beyond price. Even one thousand pounds would be too little to accept for being deprived of his companionship. Since most dog owners feel as I do on this subject, few make claims when 'Spot' goes. They have been paying their premiums for a cover they did not need.

Insuring against ill health and veterinary fees is another matter. And here, each must decide according to his means, but once again a caution: read the small print carefully to ensure you really have cover, and deal only with reputable firms and preferably take the advice of an impartial insurance broker.

15 | Responsibilities

I start this chapter by repeating something written earlier. It is that keeping a dog is not a chore. It is a simple pastime which brings an enormous amount of pleasure as payment for very modest endeavour. But this should not obscure the fact that dog ownership does entail accepting responsibilities – responsibilities to the dog; and to those both known and unknown who may have to come into contact with it.

Let's take the question of manners. Manners maketh more than man: they make dogs. Good manners, good dogs: bad manners, bad dogs. So the first responsibility you have is not to teach the dog a lot of tricks you and your acquaintances will later regret.

Briefly these consist of pulling clothes, fighting slippers, nipping at fingers, sleeping on the best settee, jumping up in welcome either with or without muddy feet, walking across the dining table, chasing cats, screaming with rage when the door bell rings and as many other similar anti-social habits as you care to imagine.

And then there is barking. Some owners, having bought a potential house guard are disappointed when he does not start work right away by barking at visitors. Asked how to encourage him to give tongue, I reply: 'Don't. His possessive instinct will develop with maturity anyway. Then your trouble may be to quieten him.'

Hark, hark, the dogs do bark, is fine if all your visitors are beggars! Mine are not, so I forbid noise; and offenders are sent to bed. Barking is a difficult habit to break. Moreover, if persistent, it's as useless a warning as was the shepherd boy's cry of 'Wolf!'

A real house dog barks only at the unusual – a scrape at a

window; a footfall after dark. Dogs do not have to be taught this; it's instinctive. All we have to do is check indiscriminate barking so that these genuine warnings are recognizable.

It is equally important to ensure that your dog does not bark when left alone in the house. While admitting that howling is even worse, both are infuriating for neighbours. Those subjected to it are entitled to complain vigorously. Dogs can and must be trained to accept occasional solitude. The lessons, however, should start not on 'cinema night' but when you are at home. Start by leaving the dog in a room on its own for five minutes. If he barks or cries, check him by banging on the door and rapping out 'No'.

Do not make the mistake of entering the room to remonstrate with him. Initially, he would rather have you there grumbling at him than be left alone. This means that you could train him to misbehave to attract your attention! The ideal training consists of demonstrating that one single 'yip' will bring a bang (a thrown tennis ball is effective) followed by marked disapproval. After five minutes quiet, call him out and reward him with pats and praise. Next day extend the period to ten minutes; then half an hour; so to an occasional hour. As much as I like dogs, I have never thought they should be able to demand my company as an absolute right for every moment of every day.

Pollution is now an issue which is of great concern to many. That means dog owners should take particular care not to offend. Clearly dogs which foul footpaths are guilty of gross pollution, and it can be avoided. Fouling of parks and other public places is also pollution. At present this is socially acceptable, but it cannot be too long before it ceases to be; then dog owners will have to take even greater precautions to avoid offending the sensibilities of others.

Hygiene in shops is another sore point which may become more inflamed in time. Nobody could defend roaming dogs in food shops; the risks are obvious. But perhaps shops should help more by installing outside pegs to which dogs could be fastened plus wire cages in which 'Toys' and other small dogs could be left.

Still on the subject of hygiene, dogs should not normally be taken into cafés, restaurants and dining-rooms and even if this is permitted they should never be allowed to eat from any plate, cup or dish used by human beings. This applies with equal force in the home.

Dogs in cars present responsibilities both to and in respect of the animal. Heaven forbid I should discourage the habit of taking dogs in cars. I rarely travel without mine. And I find her an excellent and unusually quiet back-seat driver! Conversely some dogs are less satisfactory travelling companions because they are either badly behaved, car sick or both! Let's agree there's a world of difference between one and the other. Nearly all puppies are sick when they first ride in cars but most grow out of it. Like puppyhood, even life itself, it's a complaint cured by time. Early training should start by popping the pup in the back of the car on all short shopping and station trips. Youngsters of nine weeks of age will accept cars as normal before they are adult enough to realize that travelling in them is unusual.

If, however, you had the dog before the car or if as an adult he remains a poor traveller, try a tranquillizer. But don't give it to the dog – take it yourself! Most of his trouble is brought about by your excitement; if you remain calm the dog may follow suit. There's even merit in dangling chains from back axles. Scientifically it's nonsense, but it keeps dog owners from worrying whether 'Fido' is going to be sick, so enabling him to relax and avoid it.

This problem settled, most dogs enjoy motoring. Owners can share the enjoyment only if there is a complete absence of barking, whining, jumping about and general anti-social behaviour. The answer is discipline; a continuation of that practised at home. If you are wise your dog will already 'Sit' on command in the house. See that he sits quietly in the car, and in the back seat where he cannot distract you. A counsel of perfection is that he should sit on the floor but I have never achieved this. I accept the compromise of a blanket on the back seat.

Stop dogs peering from open windows by shutting them. This prevents injury to their eyes by wind or dirt, it also stops them from deciding to jump out and greet a kerb-side friend when the car is moving!

Dogs should also be trained to stay in cars alone. Start the training at home, and once again as an extension to the 'Sit' routine. Make him sit by the car for three minutes with you out of sight. Next day repeat the lesson with him in the car and the door open. This learned, make him sit with the door shut and he will soon realize that it's not necessarily fatal to be left for a few minutes!

Still with cars, a warning which cannot be repeated too often. It is that when left in the sun cars can heat up and become death traps in a surprisingly short time. So never park in the sun if you have a dog aboard. Find some shade somehow and leave every window open an inch or so. And even then take care; one risk often forgotten is that shade is not static, it moves round with the sun.

Since cars and journeys often mean holidays, some thought should be given to the alternatives available if you cannot take your dog with you. Sometimes a temporary parting is necessary if, for example, you are going to a hotel where dogs are unacceptable or on holiday abroad.

Don't get a guilt complex over this. It's better to make proper arrangements and so have nothing to feel guilty about. If your house is occupied during your absence, leave your pet in it. Animals prefer known surroundings. Only consider boarding out if the house is to be shut.

Leaving dogs with a neighbour is only a good idea if the Samaritan is knowledgeable and really willing. A 'press-ganged' amateur is far less satisfactory than a professional.

Boarding kennels

Boarding kennel owners know about dogs. They know that innocent-faced cherub which dozes in front of your fire will behave very differently in your absence. He will probably become a potential escaper, an aggressive eater, destructive and noisy! Good kennels are prepared for this. Here's how to tell if you have chosen a good one.

Check for self-closing catches on all gates and that all staff shut every door behind them. Check that there is adequate indoor and outdoor exercise accommodation; that barriers are 'dog proof', i.e. either brick or chain link; watch the current inmates feed – if they eat up, so will yours. Forget curtain and carpet type comfort, but look for workmanlike, draught-free kennels. Welcome straw

17a Bulldog with puppies. Particularly good natured, despite terrifying appearance

17b Pug. Very fashionable in the past, now becoming popular again

18a Old English Sheepdog and puppy. An ancient working breed recently given an enormous popularity boost

18b Irish Wolfhounds. Tallest of all breeds. At one time used in Ireland for hunting wolves

19a A black and a yellow Labrador Retriever. Gentle, dependable, trainable and kind

19b Dobermanns. Very active and powerful. Not cut out for an idle existence

20a English Springer Spaniels. Twice the weight and size of the Cocker. Better suited to hedgerows than pavements

20b Cocker Spaniels. Cheerful, good tempered, busy little dogs. Love the countryside

21a Cardigan Corgi with puppies. Small, pert, rather 'bossy' dogs. Not always ideal with young children

21b Pembroke Welsh Corgi. Very trainable, easy to feed, hardy and robust

22a Afghan Hound. Quiet, dignified, very active hound. Requires space for exercise and time for daily grooming

22b Basset Hounds. Despite short legs, they often weigh upwards of 50 lb. Have appetites to match!

23a English Setter. Friendly and good natured. An excellent gundog and handsome companion

23b Boxer. Very strong, boisterous and slow to mature. Needs space indoors and out

24a Whippets. Neat, clean and elegant. Never aggressive. Happy anywhere

24b Scottish Terrier and puppies. Keen working dogs. Alert, trustworthy, affectionate

bedding which is comfortable and hygenic. Suspect the kennel which is easy going about your dog's health; they may also have been easy with a potential disease spreader. Be suspicious of those which accept your unbooked dog in mid season; the best kennels, like the best hotels, fill first.

If you are not allowed to examine the kennels by appointment, go away and stay away. The owner may be merely unsociable, but he may have something to hide. Finally, having satisfied yourself, make the booking. To postpone inspection until after your holiday is merely pretending to be a dog lover.

Dog fights

Which prompts the thought that not all dogs are dog lovers. Put another way, some of them dearly love a fight! When I was a boy I found this fact vastly stimulating – so for that matter did most other boys. Dog fights were commonplace and in most streets there was usually at least one during the twenty-four hours to brighten an otherwise dull day. We became connoisseurs. We recounted stories of the dog fights we had seen. We enlarged upon the skill and ferocity of the contestants. Some lads went even farther and openly boasted of their own particular hound's prowess in a rough and tumble. They were proud to own a dog which they variously explained as 'able to look after itself' and 'afraid of nothing'.

It is a safe assumption that those small boys were echoing the thoughts, if not the spoken words, of their parents. Probably Dad also, while not going as far as to hope his dog would fight, would certainly wear a satisfied smirk for an hour or so after it had done rather well in a chance encounter. Those days have gone. Two devastating world wars have knocked most of the fight out of us, and the dog, ever an imitator, has fallen into line.

Now we boast not that our dogs are killers but that they are kindly. Not that they are testy with others of their kind, but that they are 'good mixers'. Your dog is now 'with it' if he turns the other cheek to ill-mannered upstarts who spit and snarl. More-over, it has become fashionable to buy breeds which have no fighting background and which can be relied upon to be civilized and sociable, such as Labradors, Poodles, Pekes and Collies.

The few fights that do take place now are as often as not brought about by over anxiety on the owner's part. Grabbing at dogs to prevent a fight is a sure way of starting one. Scooping your little dog in the air is as good a way as any of encouraging a comparatively harmless acquaintance to try to jump up and bite. Putting your own dog on a lead the moment another appears in sight creates tension, as a result of which he either attempts to fight to protect you or pretends that he wants to fight knowing he is safe on the lead.

If you do have to stop a real fight, however, there are one or two things to bear in mind: firstly that if the contestants are large you cannot do it alone; that a dog with its hind legs lifted off the ground loses a lot of its drive and therefore its aggression; and finally that it's very easy to get bitten yourself – and that in the excitement it's just as likely to be your own dog which does this biting.

The best way to cool the contestants is with a well-aimed bucket of water or a well-directed hose. And I am only too well aware that these are not always available; more's the pity.

Old dogs

But the final responsibility is to the dog when he or she becomes old. This is not to say they should be treated as invalids although special measures should be taken to guard them from damp and chills. Young dogs which go to sleep with wet coats may not come to any great harm. Old dogs will probably contract rheumatism which will take all the pleasure from their lives.

Those animals which regulate their own exercise can be relied upon to curtail it themselves but very long walks for dogs over ten years of age should be avoided. Old dogs should also have their daily ration of food divided into two, and be fed morning and night; and particular care should be taken to avoid over feeding. Reduced exercise may demand a reduced diet if dangerous obesity is to be avoided.

There is one last service we can perform for all old pets and that is to decide when to save them unnecessary suffering. It is always a painful and difficult decision, but in the end your conscience must be your guide.

Appendix A

Rearing Puppies by Hand

The hand-rearing of puppies is sometimes necessary: the mother may die or become ill, her supply of milk may fail in quantity or quality or maternal care may be lacking. Whatever the reason, rapid action is necessary if the puppies are to be saved. If they are in a weak state owing to a difficult whelping or lack of milk subsequently, it is advisable to start by giving a glucose solution (1 oz glucose to 1 pint of boiled water) at blood heat every one or two hours. Healthy puppies recover rapidly and may then be given four-hourly milk feeds. Ordinary cows' milk will serve for the first few feeds but is not rich enough to support a normal rate of growth and development. Full-cream milk powder, made up at 1 part by weight to 4 parts of boiled water is richer, but too laxative owing to an excess of lactose (milk sugar).

A simple formula for household use is a preparation of $\frac{1}{2}$ oz vegetable cooking oil and 1 oz casein (Casilan or Sanatogen) dispersed in 1 pint of Jersey or Guernsey milk by stirring well and passing through a kitchen homogenizer or blender. 5–10 drops of cod liver oil may be added in the winter when the vitamin A content of cows' milk is low. Sufficient feed can be made up for about twenty-four hours and stored in a refrigerator; enough for one feed being removed when required and warmed to blood heat.

The milk feed can be given by dropper or small spoon, but much more satisfactorily by a small bottle fitted with a teat so that the puppy can suck in its instinctive manner. Suitable bottles are the 'Belcroy' Tube Feeder for premature infants supplied by John Bell and Croyden, Wigmore Street, London W.1 and the 'Catac' Foster Feeding Bottle which is available in two sizes and supplied by Cats Accessories Limited, 1 Newnham Street, Bedford.

The quantity to be given varies greatly according to the size, age and progress of the puppy. As a *very rough guide*, a new-born puppy of medium-size breed, weighing 12 oz (340 g) should take about 3 oz (85 g) of the special feed described, divided between six feeds in

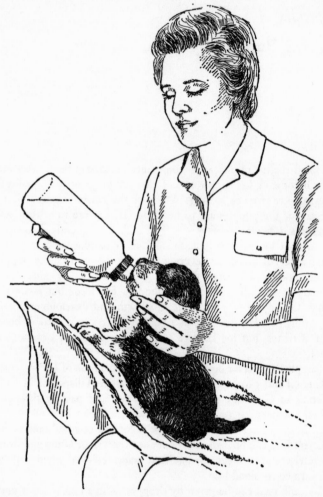

twenty-four hours. This quantity should increase rapidly, roughly in proportion to body weight, so that when weaning begins at three weeks, the puppy, now weighing at least 2 lb (900 g) will need 9 oz (255 g) or more a day divided between four feeds.

Besides correct feeding, there are two other essentials to the successful hand-rearing of puppies; warmth and the promotion of excretion.

New-born pups lose heat rapidly, cannot maintain their body temperature and lapse into a condition called hypothermia which may prove fatal unless body temperature is quickly restored. The temperature surrounding new-born pups must be maintained as near

100° F (38° C) as possible and must not fall below 90° F (32° C). If there are several pups, they should be kept together in a box with sides 6 inches (15 cm) or more high. The floor area of this box should be about twice the area covered by the puppies themselves. A light covering is useful and gentle heat supplied, for example by an electric tubular heater placed near the box. More heat must be supplied to a solitary puppy, and a small box in an airing cupboard is by no means unsuitable if the air is not too damp and also at the right temperature. The need for supplementary heat lessens as a puppy's own temperature regulating mechanism begins to work. After a week, if the pups are doing well, an ambient temperature of 75° F (24° C) is satisfactory.

A bitch nursing a litter will be seen constantly licking her young. This is not only to remove excreta and keep them clean, but also to promote excretion. When rearing by hand, it is essential to massage the abdomen of each puppy after a feed in order to stimulate both urination and defecation. The excreta should be wiped away with paper tissue or cotton wool. After about two weeks the puppy will perform without this stimulus.

Puppies raised on a bottle can be weaned in exactly the same way as those naturally reared (seepage 123 ff.). Because of the demands made by hand-rearing on time and patience, it is sensible to start weaning as early as possible, certainly by three weeks.

Appendix B

Breeds Recognised by the Kennel Club

Hound Group

Afghan Hounds
Basenjis
Basset Hounds
Bassets Griffon Vendeen
Beagles
Bloodhounds
Borzois
Deerhounds
Elkhounds
Finnish Spitz
Greyhounds
Ibizan Hounds
Irish Wolfhounds
Long-haired Dachshunds
Long-haired Miniature Dachshunds
Pharaoh Hounds
Rhodesian Ridgebacks
Salukis
Smooth-haired Dachshunds
Smooth-haired Miniature
  Dachshunds
Whippets
Wire-haired Dachshunds
Wire-haired Miniature Dachshunds

Gundog Group

American Cocker Spaniels
Chesapeake Bay Retrievers
Clumber Spaniels
Cocker Spaniels
Curly Coated Retrievers
English Setters
English Springer Spaniels
Field Spaniels
Flat Coated Retrievers
German Short-haired Pointers
Golden Retrievers
Gordon Setters
Hungarian Vizslas
Irish Setters
Irish Water Spaniels
Labrador Retrievers
Large Munsterlanders
Pointers
Sussex Spaniels
Weimaraners
Welsh Springer Spaniels

Terrier Group

Airedale Terriers
Australian Terriers
Bedlington Terriers
Border Terriers
Bull Terriers
Cairn Terriers
Dandie Dinmont Terriers
Irish Terriers
Kerry Blue Terriers
Lakeland Terriers
Manchester Terriers
Miniature Bull Terriers
Norfolk Terriers
Norwich Terriers
Scottish Terriers
Sealyham Terriers

Skye Terriers
Smooth Fox Terriers
Soft-Coated Wheaten Terriers
Staffordshire Bull Terriers
Welsh Terriers
West Highland White Terriers
Wire-haired Fox Terriers

Working Group

Alaskan Malamutes
Alsatians (German Shepherd Dogs)
Anatolian Dogs
Bearded Collies
Belgian Shepherd Dogs
  (Groenendaels)
Bernese Mountain Dogs
Boxers
Briards
Bullmastiffs
Cardigan Welsh Corgis
Dobermanns
Great Danes
Hungarian Kuvasz
Hungarian Pulis
Huskies
Maremma Italian Sheepdogs
Mastiffs
Newfoundlands
Norwegian Buhunds
Old English Sheepdogs
Pembroke Welsh Corgis
Pyrenean Mountain Dogs
Rottweilers
Rough Collies
St. Bernards
Samoyeds
Shetland Sheepdogs
Siberian Huskies
Smooth Collies

Toy Group

Cavalier King Charles Spaniels
Chinese Crested
English Toy Terriers
  (Black and Tan)
Griffons Bruxellois
Italian Greyhounds
Japanese Chin
King Charles Spaniels
Long Coat Chihuahuas
Lowchen
Maltese
Miniature Pinschers
Papillons
Pekingese
Pomeranians
Pugs
Smooth Coat Chihuahuas
Yorkshire Terriers

Utility Group

Boston Terriers
Bulldogs
Canaan Dogs
Chow Chows
Dalmatians
French Bulldogs
Giant Schnauzers
Keeshonds
Lhasa Apsos
Miniature Poodles
Miniature Schnauzers
Schipperkes
Schnauzers
Shih Tzus
Standard Poodles
Tibetan Spaniels
Tibetan Terriers
Toy Poodles

Appendix C

Breeds Recognised by the American Kennel Club

Sporting Breeds

Pointers
Pointers *(German Shorthaired)*
Pointers *(German Wirehaired)*
Retrievers *(Chesapeake Bay)*
Retrievers *(Curly-Coated)*
Retrievers *(Flat-Coated)*
Retrievers *(Golden)*
Retrievers *(Labrador)*
Setters *(English)*
Setters *(Gordon)*
Setters *(Irish)*
Spaniels *(American Water)*
Spaniels *(Brittany)*
Spaniels *(Clumber)*
Spaniels *(Cocker)*
Spaniels *(English Cocker)*
Spaniels *(English Springer)*
Spaniels *(Field)*
Spaniels *(Irish Water)*
Spaniels *(Sussex)*
Spaniels *(Welsh Springer)*
Vizslas
Weimaraners
Wirehaired Pointing Griffons

Hounds

Afghan Hounds
Basenjis
Basset Hounds
Beagles *(Thirteen inches)*
Beagles *(Fifteen inches)*

Black and Tan Coonhounds
Bloodhounds
Borzois
Dachshunds *(Longhaired)*
Dachshunds *(Smooth)*
Dachshunds *(Wirehaired)*
Foxhounds *(American)*
Foxhounds *(English)*
Greyhounds
Harriers
Irish Wolfhounds
Norwegian Elkhounds
Otter Hounds
Rhodesian Ridgebacks
Salukis
Scottish Deerhounds
Whippets

Working Breeds

Alaskan Malamutes
Belgian Malinois
Belgian Sheepdogs
Belgian Tervuren
Bernese Mountain Dogs
Bouviers des Flandres
Boxers
Briards
Bullmastiffs
Collies *(Rough)*
Collies *(Smooth)*
Dobermann Pinschers
German Shepherd Dogs
Giant Schnauzers

Great Danes
Great Pyrenees
Komondorok
Kuvaszok
Mastiffs
Newfoundlands
Old English Sheepdogs
Pulik
Rottweilers
St. Bernards
Samoyeds
Shetland Sheepdogs
Siberian Huskies
Standard Schnauzers
Welsh Corgis *(Cardigan)*
Welsh Corgis *(Pembroke)*

Terriers

Airedale Terriers
American Staffordshire Terriers
Australian Terriers
Bedlington Terriers
Border Terriers
Bull Terriers *(Coloured)*
Bull Terriers *(White)*
Cairn Terriers
Dandie Dinmont Terriers
Fox Terriers *(Smooth)*
Fox Terriers *(Wire)*
Irish Terriers
Kerry Blue Terriers
Lakeland Terriers
Manchester Terriers *(Standard)*
Miniature Schnauzers
Norwich Terriers
Scottish Terriers
Sealyham Terriers
Skye Terriers
Welsh Terriers
West Highland White Terriers

Toy Breeds

Affenpinschers

Brussels Griffons
Chihuahuas *(Long Coat)*
Chihuahuas *(Smooth Coat)*
English Toy Spaniels
Italian Greyhounds
Japanese Spaniels
Maltese
Manchester Terriers *(Toy)*
Miniature Pinschers
Papillons
Pekingese
Pomeranians
Poodles *(Toy)*
Pugs
Shih Tzu
Silky Terriers
Yorkshire Terriers

Non-Sporting Breeds

Boston Terriers
Bulldogs
Chow Chows
Dalmatians
French Bulldogs
Keeshonden
Lhasa Apsos
Poodles *(Miniature)*
Poodles *(Standard)*
Schipperkes

Miscellaneous

Akitas
Australian Cattle Dogs
Australian Kelpies
Bichon Frise
Border Collies
Cavalier King Charles Spaniels
Ibizan Hounds
Miniature Bull Terriers
Soft Coated Wheaten Terriers
Spinoni Italiani
Staffordshire Bull Terriers
Tibetan Terriers

Appendix D
Useful Items for the Dog Shelf

You may find it convenient to keep a number of items connected with the welfare of your dog together in one place. Here is a suggested list:

a. Documents

Dog Licence
Insurance Policy
Kennel Club Registration Certificate
Pedigree Certificate
Inoculation Certificates
Copy of *The Dog in the Family*

b. General care

Brush, comb and hound glove as appropriate (see Chapter 6)
Spare collar and lead
Spare engraved dog disc
Dog towel
Aerosol anti-season preparation (for bitch owners)

c. First aid & medicaments

Cotton wool
Veterinary thermometer
Teaspoon
Adhesive tape
Tincture of iodine
Flea powder

Appendix E
Useful Addresses

The Kennel Club, 1–4 Clarges Street, Piccadilly, London W1Y 8AB.

The Tail-Waggers' Club, Old Change House, Cannon Street, London EC4M 6XB.

The Royal Society for the Prevention of Cruelty to Animals, 105 Jermyn Street, London S.W.1.

Our Dogs, Oxford Road, Station Approach, Manchester M60 1SX.

Dog World, 32 New Street, Ashford, Kent.

Your local veterinary surgeon (see your telephone book)

....

Appendix F

General Dog Books

Title	Author	Publisher
Animals and the Law	T. G. Field-Fisher	U.F.A.W.
Animals Came in One by One, The	B. L. Jones	Wm. Collins & Son Ltd.
Breeding and Rearing of Dogs, The	R. H. Smythe	Popular Dogs Pub. Co. Ltd.
Care of the Family Puppy, The	Robert C. White	,,
Champion Dogs of the World	Sir R. Glyn	Harrap
Collins Guide to Dog Nutrition, The	D. R. Collins	Howell Book House
Common Sense Book of Puppy and Dog Care, The	H. Miller	Bantam Books Inc.
Complete Book of Dog Care, The	L. F. Whitney	Doubleday and Co. Inc.
Dog Breeders Introduction to Genetics	E. Frankling	Popular Dogs Pub. Co. Ltd.
Dog Breeding	F. Daglish	W. & G. Foyle Ltd.
Dog Business, The	D. Appleton	Popular Dogs Pub. Co. Ltd.
Dog Care	W. Boorer	Paul Hamlyn
Dog Owners Encyclopaedia	B. F. FitzGerald	,,
Dog Structure and Movement	R. H. Smythe	Foulsham & Co. Ltd.
Dogs	W. Boorer	Paul Hamlyn
Dogs and How to Breed Them	H. Harmar	John Gifford Ltd.
Dogs Medical Dictionary	Sewell	Routledge & Kegan Paul Ltd.
Dogs – Modern Grooming Techniques (All Breeds)	H. Harmar	John Gifford Ltd.
Dogs of the World	E. Schneider-Leyer	Popular Dogs Pub. Co. Ltd.
Expert Obedience Training for Dogs	G. Strickland	Barrie & Jenkins Ltd.
Family Dog, The	J. Holmes	Popular Dogs Pub. Co. Ltd.
Farmer's Dog, The	,,	,,
Feeding of Dogs, The	J. T. Abrams	W. Green of Edinburgh
First Aid and Nursing	Edgson/ Gwynne-Jones	Popular Dogs Pub. Co. Ltd.
First Aid for your Dog		W. & G. Foyle Ltd.
Genetics and the Social Behaviour of the Dog	J. P. Scott	University of Chicago Press

Title	Author	Publisher
Genetics of the Dog	Burns/Fraser	Oliver & Boyd Ltd.
Gundogs: Training and Field Trials	P. Moxon	Popular Dogs Pub. Co. Ltd.
International Encyclopaedia of Dogs, The	Stanley Dangerfield and Elizabeth Howell	Pelham Boooks
Kennel Buildings and Plans	W. Judy	Judy Publishing Co.
Mating and Whelping of Dogs, The	R.Portman-Graham	Popular Dogs Pub. Co. Ltd.
Obedience and Security Training for Dogs	T. Scott	Popular Dogs Pub. Co. Ltd.
Odd Dogs	M. Daly	W. & R. Chambers Ltd.
Perfect Dog Owner, The	S. Dangerfield	Museum Press
Pointers and Setters	W. Marr	Privately Published
Police Dogs – Training and Care		H.M.S.O.
Popular Guide to Puppy Rearing	O. Gwynne-Jones	Popular Dogs Pub. Co. Ltd.
Practical Dog Breeding and Genetics	E. Frankling	,,
Practical Guide to Showing Dogs	Portman-Graham	,,
Private Life of the Dog: Does it Think	R. H. Smythe	Foulsham & Co. Ltd.
Showing your Dog	L. Perrins	W. & G. Foyle Ltd.
Spaniel Owners' Encyclopaedia	J. Gordon	Pelham Books Ltd.
Talking about Dogs	S. Dangerfield	Barrie Books
Toy Breeds, The	Sheldon/Lockwood	Pelham Books Ltd.
Train Your Own Labrador	E. Beck	George Newnes Ltd.
Training the Retriever: A Manual	J. Kersley	Popular Dogs Pub. Co. Ltd.
Training Your Dog	F. Daglish	W. & G. Foyle Ltd.
Why does Your Dog do that?	S. Bergman	Popular Dogs Pub. Co. Ltd.
You and your Dog	S. Dangerfield	Barrie Books
You and your Puppy	,,	,,

Books on Breeds

Afghan Hound, The	Harrison	Popular Dogs Pub. Co. Ltd.
Airedale Terrier, Handbook	Hayes	W. & G. Foyle Ltd.
Alsatian, Handbook	L. Leonard	W. & G. Foyle Ltd.
Alsatian Owners' Encyclopaedia	Pickup	Pelham Books Ltd.
Alsatian, The	Schwabacher/Gray	Popular Dogs Pub. Co. Ltd.
American Cocker Spaniel	Kraeuchi	Judy Publishing Co.
Basset Hound, Handbook	F. Daglish	W. & G. Foyle Ltd.
Complete Alsatian, The	N. Elliot	Kaye & Ward Ltd.
Modern Bloodlines in Alsatian	N. Elliot	,,
Basset Hound, The	G. Johnston	Popular Dogs Pub. Co. Ltd.
Beagle, Handbook	F. Daglish	W. & G. Foyle Ltd.
Beagle, The	T. Gray	Popular Dogs Pub. Co. Ltd.
Beagles and Beagling	D. C. Appleton	Kaye & Ward Ltd.
Bloodhound, Handbook	H. Harmar	W. & G. Foyle Ltd.

Title	Author	Publisher
Bloodhound, Handbook	D. Appleton	Dog Lovers Library
Border Terrier, Handbook	Irving	W. & G. Foyle Ltd.
Boston Terrier, The	V. Berry	Judy Publishing Co.
Boxer, Handbook	C. Wilson-Wiley	W. & G. Foyle Ltd.
Boxer, Handbook	J. Dunkels	Dog Lovers Library
Boxers, All About	J. Gordon	Pelham Books Ltd.
Boxer, The	E. Somerfield	Popular Dogs Pub. Co. Ltd.
Boxer, The	D. Gordon	Judy Publishing Co.
My Life with Boxers	F. Stockmann	Popular Dogs Pub. Co. Ltd.
Of Dogs and Duty	D. Johnson	Privately Published (Dist. by K. & R. Books Ltd.)
Bullmastiff, Handbook	C. Hubbard	Dog Lovers Library
Bull Terrier, Forty Years of	G. Adlam	Dog World Ltd.
Bull Terrier, A History	Oppenheimer	"
After Bar Sinister	"	"
Cairn Terrier, Handbook	Whitehead	W. & G. Foyle Ltd.
Cairn Terrier, The	Beynon/Fisher	Popular Dogs Pub. Co. Ltd.
Cavalier King Charles Spaniel	Stenning	W. & G. Foyle Ltd.
Cavalier King Charles Spaniel, The	M. Forwood	Popular Dogs Pub. Co. Ltd.
Chihuahua, Handbook	H. Harmar	W. & G. Foyle Ltd.
Dobermann, The	Curnow/Faulks	Popular Dogs Pub. Co. Ltd.
Springer Spaniel, The	Hooper/Hampton	"
Your Poodle and Mine	S. Dangerfield	Barrie Books

Index